HTML5
GAME ENGINES
App Development and Distribution

HTML5
GAME ENGINES
App Development and Distribution

Dan Nagle

CRC Press
Taylor & Francis Group
Boca Raton London New York

CRC Press is an imprint of the
Taylor & Francis Group, an **informa** business

AN A K PETERS BOOK

CRC Press
Taylor & Francis Group
6000 Broken Sound Parkway NW, Suite 300
Boca Raton, FL 33487-2742

First issued in hardback 2018

© 2014 by Taylor & Francis Group, LLC
CRC Press is an imprint of Taylor & Francis Group, an Informa business

No claim to original U.S. Government works

ISBN 13: 978-1-138-42836-2 (hbk)
ISBN 13: 978-1-4665-9400-5 (pbk)

Visit the Taylor & Francis Web site at
http://www.taylorandfrancis.com

and the CRC Press Web site at
http://www.crcpress.com

To my parents,
Randall and Karen Nagle.

Contents

Preface

HTML5 is rapidly gaining in popularity. Because it is based on browser technology, and just about every device has a browser, just about every device can run HTML5. An app written in HTML5 can run on Windows, Mac, Linux, Android, iOS, and more, as new devices are released. Being able to write an app once and then publish it to nearly all gadget and computer owners is very appealing.

Currently, HTML5 is a popular platform in mobile app markets for simple apps. As mobile hardware improves, HTML5 is starting to be used for gaming apps, and there is a growing industry of game engines to support it. This book is an introduction to development with HTML5 game engines, an in-depth look at some popular engines, downloadable example projects for each engine, and techniques on how to package and distribute the final app to all the major platforms.

How to Use This Book

This book is divided into three main parts. Each part has a specific goal.

Part I: HTML5 Game Development
If you have limited HTML5 development experience or would like a refresher, then Part I is the place to start. It covers HTML5 starting with the essentials and completing with a basic pong game running in the browser with no dependencies. Along the way, HTML5 development strategies and techniques are discussed.

Part II: HTML5 Game Engines
Part II implements four different games using four different game engines. The engines and games covered include:

1. The **Crafty** (http://craftyjs.com/) game engine is used to create **Crafty Pong** based on the basic HTML5 pong game developed in Part I. Unlike Part I, the engine-powered version uses graphics, sounds, touch controls, mouse controls, and animations.

2. **EaselJS** (http://www.createjs.com/#!/EaselJS) along with the CreateJS suite is used to create a basic **Tic-Tac-Toe** game. The engine itself is used to draw dynamic graphics and respond to events. The game also plays sounds.

3. The **Impact** (http://impactjs.com/) game engine is used to create **MechaJet**, a two-level action side-scroller. It features graphics, sounds, physics, animation, HUD, touch controls ... essentially the workings of a feature-complete HTML5 game.

4. The **Turbulenz** (http://turbulenz.com/) game engine is used to create **Sky Marble**, a puzzle-style physics game. It covers many of the complex areas of MechaJet plus adds 3D elements to the game.

Part III: HTML5 App Distribution
Once the app is built, the next step is to distribute it. Several of the games created in Part II are used as examples for distribution in **Chrome Web Store, Apple iOS App Store, Google Play Store,**

Facebook, and finally distribution with **Native Windows** and **Native Mac** installers.

The book can be read from start to finish with each chapter building on top of the other. However, the book was also designed so that, if you have specific goals in mind, you can jump to that particular chapter to read about the presented example. Though the book may reference techniques from earlier chapters, all the examples were intentionally built independently to support this strategy.

Once your game with your choice of engine is finished, you can work through Part III on techniques to get your game into all the different app markets you wish to target. For example, if **Impact** is your engine of choice, consider this reading strategy:

Part I (if you want a refresher) → Part II (just Impact section) → Part III (the different markets you wish to cover).

Not all the examples are placed in all the app markets, but the techniques among the different engines are very similar. Finally, there is a section at the end of the book called Tools Appendix on page 175. HTML5 game development can require a very wide variety of tools. Rather than give each one a formal introduction, the minor tools were placed in this appendix.

All the source code and examples are available at the website http:// HTML5GameEnginesBook.com/. All the code, graphics, and sound are licensed free for personal and commercial use (MIT and CC-BY-3.0). The game engines and other tools are distributed with respect to their licenses.

About the Author

Since graduating *magna cum laude* in Computer Engineering from Mississippi State University in 2003, **Dan Nagle** has worked with numerous software platforms and architectures and has written apps for Android, Windows, Mac, Linux, iOS, numerous web apps, network servers, and pure embedded C.

For about four years, he owned and operated a web company focused on website hosting and custom game development. Before that, he was an electrical engineer developing embedded systems.

Currently, Dan Nagle is a senior software engineer writing control software and web interfaces for network devices distributing HD video. He can be reached through his website at http://DanNagle.com/

Acknowledgments

I would like to thank everybody at CRC Press for their help. I would particularly like to thank my editor, Rick Adams, for being very flexible during this project as it is chasing a very fast-moving industry. I would like to thank my wife, Karen, for all her support with my various ventures. Finally, I would like to thank Philip Rideout, Jerry McMahan, and Michael Rutledge for their help with proofreading.

Part I

HTML5 Game Development

Chapter 1

Introduction to HTML5

1.1 The HTML5 Standard

The HTML5 standard is located at http://www.whatwg.org/html [6]. If you are looking for an authoritative answer to a question related to HTML5, you can find it there. Unlike many specification documents, this standard is actually well organized, readable, and up to date. Unfortunately, this standard has a competing standard located at http://www.w3.org/TR/html5/ [7].

Why are there two standards? This chapter explains a little HTML5 history on how this came to be.

1.1.1 A Brief History of HTML

HTML (HyperText Markup Language) was originally developed by Sir Tim Berners-Lee (credited as the inventor of the World Wide Web) around 1990 during his work at CERN [19]. He called it "HTML Tags". The World Wide Web Consortium (W3C) was later founded by Berners-Lee and continued to maintain the standard. It went through a few iterations (HTML+, HTML 2.0, etc) and eventually formally standardized as HTML 4 in 1997. After some maintenance and edits, it became HTML 4.01 in late 1999 [9].

Rather than continue to extend and polish HTML 4, the W3C took a sharp turn and started developing XHTML and published version 1.0 in 2001 [10]. XHTML made HTML an extension of XML instead of its normal roots as an extension of Standard Generalized Markup Language (SGML). Despite many good ideas in XHTML (enforcing well-formed documents), the idea was dead before it left the door. Old pages weren't compatible without some serious revising (and web servers needed reconfiguring, too—pages need to be sent as "XML" instead of "HTML", a step very commonly left out). Therefore,

3

companies saw no tangible benefits, and not wanting to revise a bunch of pages, many stayed with tried-and-true HTML 4.

In 2004, W3C was working on XHTML2 [11] that was not compatible with either HTML or XHTML [12]. Representatives from Mozilla, Opera, and Apple decided to join together because they saw the XHTML standard presenting a very document-centric Internet. This new group wanted HTML standards that supported their needs: developing web applications. Therefore, they formed WHATWG (**W**eb **H**ypertext **A**pplication **T**echnology **W**orking **G**roup). They began work on what would eventually be called HTML5 [13].

In 2012, the W3C relented and adopted WHATWG's specification for HTML5. Unfortunately, the story does not end with a happy collaboration of WHATWG and W3C working to better the web for everybody. In mid-2012, the two organizations split when W3C wanted to see the specification reach completion, and WHATWG declared HTML5 to be a living document [14]. There has already been some minor divergence (such as whether the title tag is actually required). Which "standard" does a developer follow? Good question. For now, WHATWG has strong backing of the browser maintainers (Mozilla (Gecko), Apple (Webkit), Opera (formerly Presto, now Blink)) that actually implement the standard. Therefore, their statements should take precedence.

1.2   HTML5, the New Living Standard

HTML5 was considered "complete" by the W3C on December 17, 2012 [7]. As of early 2014, it was not yet considered finalized. However, browser manufacturers have already implemented significant parts of HTML5. Informally, HTML5 encompasses these new technologies:

- Canvas

- CSS3

- Device API

- File API

- Geolocation

- Microdata

- SVG

- Web SQL Database **(Removed in late 2010)**

- Web Sockets

- Web Storage

- Web Workers

- WebGL

Not all sections are technically part of HTML5 (such as CSS3, and to some extent, WebGL). However, many parts that make HTML5 attractive to developers rely on them, so they are included for convenience. Web SQL Database was on the road map, but has been abandoned [15]. It is listed above because some books mention it, and since HTML5 is now a living standard, it could be put back.

The feature that you should become most familiar with as an HTML5 game developer is Canvas. No longer are you constrained to performing DOM(document object model) tricks on the browser page to make a game. With Canvas, you draw animated graphics directly. The other major addition that makes games for HTML5 possible is audio. Audio is now a first class citizen (no "embed" tag needed). Finally, the last addition covered in this book is WebGL. WebGL acts as a gateway to OpenGL to create some truly impressive games.

1.3 HTML5 Stands Alone

Back in 1995, when the web started really coming to prominence, a piece of technology took off that promised to allow developers to "write once, run everywhere." That technology was called Java [1]. The idea is that there is no need to worry about the underlying components of the operating system running the app. Java compiles the app to "byte code," which is then passed to the "Java Virtual Machine" for final execution on any supported platform with a Java Runtime Environment. The hype surrounding this new technology is part of what drives the (perhaps conspiracy) theory that JavaScript was given the unfortunate name *Java*Script purely to ride the coattails of Java. Regardless of the reason, developers are now required to constantly explain to non-developers that JavaScript != Java. Since then, Java "applets" have been hard to find because they are large, clumsy, and simply not a pleasant experience for the user. The Java applet went away in favor of a new contender: Flash.

The reason Flash replaced the Java applet so quickly [4] is because it actually worked well. It was quick and provided a seamless experience for the end user. Years later, Adobe Flash is still used everywhere except for one very important area: Mobile. Flash was never supported in iOS, and as of 2011, Adobe no longer supports Flash on Android [5].

Shortly after Adobe dropped support for Flash in Android, Apple declared Java a deprecated technology and no longer ships it with Mac OS X [3]. With Java deprecated from Apple products and Flash support waning for mobile, HTML5 now stands alone as the one high-level platform that can target the top computing platforms.

1.4   Source Code

All of the source code and examples are available at the website http://HTML5GameEnginesBook.com/. All the code, graphics, and sound is licensed free for personal and commercial use (MIT and CC-BY-3.0).

1.5   A Touch of Game Design

Before beginning development of HTML5 Pong, I invite you to read the Tools Appendix on page 175. It contains descriptions of various tools needed for HTML5 development. Critical tools will get a formal introduction as needed, while tools that are important, but not necessarily the focus of this book (e.g., Git,) are delegated to that appendix for reference.

Now that we have been introduced to HTML5, we are ready to put it to practice. For this, we are going to develop Pong, which is what I consider to be the "Hello World" for video game development. Normally, at this stage of the book, an introduction to game design principles would be presented. However, we are all already familiar with Pong, and this is just a learning exercise, so there is no need for the detailed design document. A problem statement will do:

> "Pong is a minimalistic 1-player HTML5-based game with 2 paddles and a ball that reverses directions on collisions."

Problem statements are very useful in game design. Simply forming a succinct sentence to get to the essence of the goal can bring clarity. For more complex games and applications, a design document is often used. Rather than a formal design document, I recommend setting up a private wiki as the design document so it can be a living document that grows as the game is developed.

Game design is an art and skill that can take years of practice and to master. This book is not about game design as there are already a number of very good books on the subject. This book is about HTML5 game development and operates under the assumption that you already have a general idea of the kind of game you want to make.

1.6　HTML5 Hello World Canvas

Before starting on Pong, we must learn "Hello World." Listing 1.1 is the
minimum amount of HTML code required to generate a "Hello World" on
a Canvas element. It is the starting point of our Pong game. Its output in
Chrome is shown in Figure 1.1.

```
<!doctype html>
<html lang="en">
<head>
    <meta charset="UTF-8">
    <title>Hello World!</title>
</head>
<script>
function onload() {
  var canvas=document.getElementById("canvas");
  var context=canvas.getContext("2d");
    context.font = 'bold 30px Times';
  context.fillText("Hello World!", canvas.width / 3,
    canvas.height / 3);
}
</script>
<body onload="onload()">
    <canvas id="canvas" width="320" height="480"></canvas>
</body>
</html>
```

Listing 1.1. HTML5 Hello World Canvas.

Figure 1.1. HTML5 Hello World Canvas Chrome.

This "Hello World!" does not really showcase HTML5. The same could be
done using normal DIV elements from HTML 4. Let's make it more HTML5-
like. Look at the code in Listing 1.2 and the result in Figure 1.2. This result
is much more interesting.

```
<!doctype html>
<html lang="en">
<head>
    <meta charset="UTF-8">
    <title>Hello World</title>
</head>
<script>
function onload() {
  var canvas=document.getElementById("canvas");
  var context=canvas.getContext("2d");
    context.font = 'bold 30px Times';
  context.fillText("Hello World!", canvas.width / 3,
    canvas.height / 3);
}
</script>
<body onload="onload()">
    <canvas id="canvas" width="320"
        height="480">Sorry!</canvas>
</body>
</html>
```

Listing 1.2. HTML5 Hello World angled.

Figure 1.2. HTML5 Hello World Canvas Chrome angled.

Here is a line-by-line explanation of what is happening:

<!doctype html>

> This is the HTML5 document type declaration (DTD). It is required
> for all HTML5-based web pages. There is no versioning as HTML5 is a
> living standard.

> This is a welcome change from the numerous document declarations. For
> example, HTML 4.01 Transitional required this at the top of every page.

```
<!DOCTYPE HTML PUBLIC "-//W3C//DTD HTML 4.01 Transitional//EN"
   "http://www.w3.org/TR/html4/loose.dtd">
```

Do not leave off your document type declarations. Though Firefox and Chrome are very tolerant, you could get strange behaviors from Internet Explorer. IE has many different rendering modes (strict, loose, IE8-compatible, etc.), and without a DTD, the one it chooses is difficult to predict.

`<html lang="en">`

This sets the language to English. There is no language default in HTML5, so you should specify one.

`<head>`

Start of header. This section contains special metadata about the document (such as the title).

`<meta charset="UTF-8">`

Even if you are using no special characters, you should declare that you are using UTF-8 as your character encoding. Some versions of IE have known security vulnerabilities if UTF-8 is left off. Without it, IE or other browsers may treat your encoding as UTF-7 (an extended version of plain ASCII).

`<title >Hello World </title >`

Title of the page. The WHATWG standard says this is optional, but the W3C standard says this is required for all HTML documents. For your purposes, you should require it because various features of web browsers rely on it (such as bookmarks). Also, a good title is extremely important for Search Engine Optimization (SEO).

`<script>`

The phrase `type='text/javascript'` is no longer required in HTML5. All browsers will assume JavaScript. These type attributes are a holdover from XHTML, which required them. Actually, you would do best to avoid it completely because a typo in the attribute could cause the browser to not read it correctly since specifying type overrides its default assumptions. Note that using just `<style>` is acceptable for CSS as well.

`var canvas=document.getElementById("canvas");`

Fetch the element with `id="canvas"`. Store it in a variable.

`var context=canvas.getContext("2d");`

I am using a 2D canvas. HTML5 supports a 3D canvas, but support is still very limited. 3D will be covered in Chapter 6.

`context.font = 'bold 30px Times';`

Set the font designation.

`context.rotate(Math.PI/4);`

> I am now rotating the canvas 45 degrees; `rotate()` uses radians to measure angles. Math.PI is the JavaScript constant for PI.

`context.fillText("Hello World!", canvas.width/4, 0);`

> I am now writing the text to x and y coordinates. I use width of the canvas divided by 4 to make it more in the middle of the canvas block.

`context.restore();`

> I am now restoring the canvas from its rotation. This leaves the "Hello World!" at an angle. Note that to the viewer, it appears I operated solely on the text. What I actually did was rotate the entire canvas, write the text normally, and then restore the orientation of the canvas. Rotate-write-restore is a very common technique in graphics programming.

`<body onload="onload()">`

> This tells the browser to execute the custom onload function after the page has finished loading. This is important because I want the canvas available before I begin using it.

`<canvas id="canvas" width="320" height="480">Sorry!</canvas>`

> This sets up my HTML5 canvas block. A browser that didn't support canvas would display the inner text or possibly leave it blank.

Like many examples of "Hello World!", we could take a different path. If all we wanted was rotated text, we could turn the canvas into `<div id="mytext">Hello World!</div>` and just use the CSS3 transform property. No JavaScript needed. See Listing 1.3 for the example code and Figure 1.3 for the output.

```
<!doctype html>
<html lang="en">
<head>
    <meta charset="UTF-8">
    <title>HTML5 Hello World CSS Angled</title>
</head>
<style>
#mytext
{
font-weight:bold;
font-size:30px;
font-family:"Times",Georgia,Serif;
transform:rotate(45deg); /*Non-prefixed future versions*/
-ms-transform:rotate(45deg); /* IE */
-moz-transform:rotate(45deg); /* Firefox */
-webkit-transform:rotate(45deg); /* Safari and Chrome */
-o-transform:rotate(45deg); /* Opera*/
position: absolute;
top: 100px;
```

```
left: 50px;
}
</style>
<body>
    <div id="mytext" width="320"
         height="480">Hello World!</canvas>
</body>
</html>
```

Listing 1.3. HTML5 Hello World CSS angled.

Figure 1.3. HTML5 Hello World CSS angled Chrome.

There are lots of new features with CSS3, enough to make a game in its own right. CSS3 transitions and translate are really nice, and using these built-in effects usually means hardware-level optimization by the browser manufacturers and less work for you. The old way of performing effects required manually moving elements by iterating over their x/y or other style values over time. This can be inefficient and sometimes look jagged. If you can find a CSS3 way of doing things, you should favor it.

1.7   Pong Game Board

We are now ready for Pong. To get started, we will draw the game board. To start with, it will be sufficient to just color the pieces. We also will leave the screen at 320x480. This is the same resolution as the first few generations of iPhone and Android devices [32]. Refer to the Canvas-based HTML file mentioned earlier. For now, the only difference is changes to the `onload()` function.

Look at Listing 1.4 for the HTML5 code to draw the paddles, background, and ball for our HTML5 Pong. For clarity, the header is omitted. The output is in Figure 1.4 .

```
function onload() {
  var canvas=document.getElementById("canvas");
  var context=canvas.getContext("2d");

  context.fillStyle = '#dbdbdb';  //color for rectangle

  //draw rectangle
  context.fillRect(0, 0, canvas.width, canvas.height);

  context.fillStyle = '#000000';  //color for inside shapes

  context.fillRect(100,10,100,10); // draw top paddle

  context.strokeStyle = '#000000';  //color for ball
  context.beginPath();  //start a draw path

  // draw ball
  context.arc(canvas.width / 2,canvas.height / 2,10,0,
    Math.PI*2,true);

  context.fill(); //close path and fill in the shape

  // draw bottom paddle
  context.fillRect(100,canvas.height - 20,100,10);
}
```

Listing 1.4. HTML5 Pong Static Board.

Figure 1.4. HTML5 Pong Static Board Chrome.

1.8 Pong Game Loop

Right now, our game is a static image. All games have what is called a "game loop." These perform animations, background calculations, essentially anything needed to keep the game running. Our game needs a game loop.

To do that in HTML5, we use a JavaScript function called `setInterval()`. See below:

```
var gameFPS = 30; // Our game will run at 30 frames per second
window.setInterval(pongGame, 1000 / gameFPS); //start game loop
```

"FPS" is "frames per second" and is also called "frame rate." The final rendering of each redraw of the game is called a *frame*. Each time the game begins traversal through the game logic, this is called a "frame tick." For a good idea on what is a good frame rate, consider that up until *The Hobbit: An Unexpected Journey* (2012) was released, nearly all movies were filmed at 24 FPS. *The Hobbit* was filmed at 48 FPS [33]. Most monitors can handle up to 60 FPS. With these stats at hand, a good benchmark for game developers should be a minimum of 30 FPS.

The HTML5 specification states a minimum `setInterval()` of 4 ms [8]. That is 250 FPS. Note that a hard-coded frame rate is not good game design. You would rather the game gets drawn as fast as the hardware can handle and adjust your game logic accordingly. If the game can run at 60 FPS, why stop it? Also, there is no guarantee that the device that plays your game can handle 30 FPS, which means `pongGame()` could get called before the previous frame is finished (though unlikely because JavaScript is single-threaded, but that is not guaranteed either).

Some of the problems with `setInterval()` are solved with the more modern `requestAnimationFrame()` function. Instead of a hard-coded target frame rate, `requestAnimationFrame()` tells the browser to update the screen at the next convenient opportunity. The browser recognizes this function as animation and optimizes accordingly (such as waiting until the entire frame is finished and updating the final image at once versus individual elements).

Fortunately, the game engines we are going to look at in Part II manage `requestAnimationFrame()`, `setInterval()`, and other game loop decisions for you. For our learning exercise for this simple game, a hard-coded rate with `setInterval()` is fine.

1.9 Pong Game Refactoring

HTML5 Canvas uses immediate mode bit-mapped rendering [34]. This means that objects are drawn immediately (no double buffering), and the result is a single graphical image (no objects). This is different from Flash. Flash uses retained mode and objects [35]. It keeps objects in memory and draws them when attributes change. With HTML5 Canvas, there is no Flash timeline and no display lists. The closest equivalent is Flash Stage. There are pros and cons to each strategy, which can make a nice lively debate that won't be covered here. Regardless, we are using HTML5 Canvas, so we need to refactor our

pong game so it redraws the entire scene every frame. See Listing 1.5 for the
initial round of refactoring. All the major components and logic have been
reorganized into functions.

```
var gameFPS = 30; // Our game will run at 30 frames per second
var canvas=document.getElementById("canvas");
var context=canvas.getContext("2d");

function drawBackground() {
  context.fillStyle = '#dbdbdb';  //color for rectangle

  //draw rectangle
  context.fillRect(0, 0, canvas.width, canvas.height);
}
function drawBall() {
  context.strokeStyle = '#000000';  //color for ball
  context.beginPath();  //start a draw path
  context.arc(160,240,10,0,Math.PI*2,true); // draw ball
  context.fill(); //close path and fill in the shape

}
function drawTopPaddle() {
  context.fillStyle = '#000000';  //color for inside shapes
  context.fillRect(100,10,100,10); // draw top paddle
}
function drawBottomPaddle() {
  context.fillStyle = '#000000';  //color for inside shapes
  context.fillRect(100,460,100,10); // draw top paddle
}
function pongGame() {
  drawBackground();
  drawTopPaddle();
  drawBottomPaddle();
  drawBall();
}
  //start game loop
window.setInterval(pongGame, 1000 /  gameFPS);
```

Listing 1.5. HTML5 Pong First Refactor.

This will render the same screen as before in Figure 1.4. The difference is
our code is better organized so we can manage changes to the background, ball,
and paddles. Notice the ordering. Since the end result is a single graphical
image, whatever gets drawn last is layered at the top. That means our ball
will get drawn on top of the paddles if we are not careful.

Now, let us make the game do something. We will start with the ball
bouncing around. Every frame, the ball should move, and it should bounce off
of walls. See Listing 1.6 for this update to the code.

```
var ball = new Object();
ball['x'] = 160; ball['y'] = 240;
ball['xspeed'] = 1; ball['yspeed'] = 3;

function drawBall()
{
   context.strokeStyle = '#000000';  //color for ball
   context.beginPath();  //start a draw path
   ball.x += ball.xspeed;
   ball.y += ball.yspeed;
   context.arc(ball.x,ball.y,10,0,Math.PI*2,true); // draw ball
   context.fill(); //close path and fill in the shape

   if(ball.x >= canvas.width || ball.x <= 0 ) {
     ball.xspeed = ball.xspeed * -1;
   }

   if(ball.y >= canvas.height || ball.y <= 0 ) {
     ball.yspeed = ball.yspeed * -1;
   }
}
```

Listing 1.6. HTML5 Pong Game Ball Bounce.

The ball was pulled out of the update function and given variables to track location and speed. Now the ball will bounce around the screen forever moving at one pixel every frame. The variable `yspeed` was set to 3 to give the ball a bit more downward motion since the game board is tall. Depending on which edge, it will reverse the direction of one of its speed variables.

However, we only want the ball to reverse course if it hits the side walls or a paddle. It is not enough to just look at the canvas coordinates. To achieve this, we need to add hit detection. Some goals we need to solve with the hit detection include:

1. Ball reverses vertical motion if it hits a paddle.

2. Ball reverses horizontal motion if it hits a wall.

3. Ball bounces on its surface (instead of the center point).

Let us add a function called `hitDetect()` that performs the various hit detections for our ball. Like all functions that need repeated calls, it will go in `pongGame()`. See Listing 1.7. This is a meaty example. Don't get too concerned about the numerous additions and subtractions.

```
function hitDetect()
{
  if((ball.y +BALL_RADIUS)  >= (bottomPaddle.y))
  {
    if(bottomPaddle.x <= ball.x && ball.x <=
      (bottomPaddle.x + PADDLE_WIDTH))
    {
      console.log("bottomPaddle hit", ball.x, ball.y,
      bottomPaddle.x, bottomPaddle.y);
      ball.yspeed = ball.yspeed * -1;
      ball.y = bottomPaddle.y - BALL_RADIUS;
      return;
    }
  }
  if((ball.y -BALL_RADIUS) <= (topPaddle.y+PADDLE_HEIGHT))
  {
    if(topPaddle.x <= ball.x && ball.x <=
      (topPaddle.x + PADDLE_WIDTH))
    {
      console.log("topPaddle hit", ball.x, ball.y,
      topPaddle.x, topPaddle.y);
      ball.yspeed = ball.yspeed * -1;
      ball.y = topPaddle.y + BALL_RADIUS+PADDLE_HEIGHT;
      return;
    }
  }
  if((ball.x + BALL_RADIUS) >= canvas.width
    || (ball.x - BALL_RADIUS) <= 0 )
  {
    ball.xspeed = ball.xspeed * -1;
  }
  if(ball.y > (canvas.height + BALL_RADIUS)
    || ball.y < (0 -  BALL_RADIUS) )
  {
    initGameObjects();
  }
}
```

Listing 1.7. HTML5 Pong Game hit detect.

The code in Listing 1.7 has some additional refactoring.

- Paddles are now objects with location variables for easy tracking.

- Paddle width and height is now PADDLE_ WIDTH and PADDLE_HEIGHT.

- The radius of the ball is now BALL_RADIUS.

The logic becomes more complex depending on if the ball is at the top, left, bottom, or right portions of the screen. PADDLE_WIDTH, PADDLE_HEIGHT, and BALL_RADIUS are added and subtracted as needed so the collision occurs on the surface of the ball.

Also, notice after the bounce the `ball.y` value is forced outside the paddle. This covers the case of the user sliding the paddle into the side of the ball. Without this, the ball could get "stuck" inside the paddle as it toggles direction rapidly.

Finally, you can see `console.log()` statements. These values are outputted to the chrome debugger (or the Firefox debugger). The `console.log()` function is an invaluable tool for run-time troubleshooting.

Next, we need to let the user control the paddle. The player will control the bottom paddle using the keyboard. Left arrow will move the paddle left. Right arrow will move the paddle right. To do this, we bind the keyboard event and track which key was hit. Then the input will be applied during the next frame tick as appropriate.

See below for the keyboard binding. A very easy way to find correct key codes is to simply drop the event into `console.log()`:

```
document.onkeydown = function(event){
    console.log(event.keyCode); //what key did I press?
    if(event.keyCode == 39) //right arrow
    {
        rightArrowHit = true;
    }
    if(event.keyCode == 37) //left arrow
    {
        leftArrowHit = true;
    }
}
```

We now need to add `keyboardEvents` to our `pongGame()` function. See below:

```
function keybardEvents()
{
    if(leftArrowHit)
    {
        bottomPaddle.x -= 3;
        leftArrowHit = false;
    }
    if(rightArrowHit)
    {
        bottomPaddle.x += 3;
        rightArrowHit = false;
    }
    if(bottomPaddle.x <= 0)
    {
        bottomPaddle.x = 0;
    }
    if(bottomPaddle.x >= (canvas.width - PADDLE_WIDTH))
    {
        bottomPaddle.x = canvas.width - PADDLE_WIDTH;
    }
}
```

Now, the player can move the paddle around and bounce the ball. The next step is having the computer control the top paddle. All artificial intelligence can go in a function called `computerAI()` that gets called with our other functions inside `pongGame()`. See below for the computer AI.

```
function computerAI()
{
  if(ball.yspeed < 0)
  {
    if(ball.x < (topPaddle.x + PADDLE_WIDTH / 2))
    {
      topPaddle.x--;
    } else {
      topPaddle.x++;
    }
  }
  if(topPaddle.x <= 0)
  {
    topPaddle.x = 0;
  }
  if(topPaddle.x >= (canvas.width - PADDLE_WIDTH))
  {
    topPaddle.x = canvas.width - PADDLE_WIDTH;
  }
}
```

Our AI is very simple. It tries to center its paddle on the ball, and it only moves when the ball is traveling toward it. It also moves slower than the player (just one pixel per frame). This will be a very easy game, but it works well enough for our demo.

Now, our game just needs a score. We can write the text in the top left corner. It will get updated in our `pongGame()` loop. See below for the score function:

```
var pointsPlayer = 0;
var pointsComputer = 0;

function drawScore()
{
  if(pointsPlayer > 0 || pointsComputer > 0)
  {
    context.font = 'bold 15px Times';
    context.fillText("You:" + pointsPlayer
      +"  CPU:" + pointsComputer, 5, 12);
  }
}
```

Not shown is the updated `hitDetect()` function that increments the player or computer score when the ball goes off-screen. All of the added functions get executed during each frame tick. Below is the final list of functions executed by `pongGame()`.

```
function pongGame() {

    keybardEvents();
    computerAI();
    drawBackground();
    drawTopPaddle();
    drawBottomPaddle();
    drawBall();
    hitDetect();
    drawScore();

}
```

To clarify, every 1/30 of a second (30 FPS), the JavaScript engine executes `pongGame()` via `setInterval()`. Inside `pongGame()`, keyboard events were captured between frames. We then process the computer AI. With the internal stats updated, we then draw the background, top paddle, bottom paddle, and ball. We then perform hit detection, and finally we draw the score on top of everything else. You are invited to rearrange the order or comment out these functions to see what happens.

1.10   Summary

We have a "complete" game written purely in HTML5. We have player control, AI control, and a score. The game is a bit dull, though. Sprinkling some random values in various places (like the start location of the ball) could help. Also, mobile users are completely left out. They cannot control the game because mobile devices do not have left/right arrows. As soon as they load the page, the ball will immediately go off the board. Finally, what is a game without some graphics and sound? Once you start adding these requirements, you will need to learn some more complex techniques, which brings us to the next chapter.

Chapter 2

HTML5 Development Strategies

In the previous chapter, we created a very basic HTML5 Pong game. The entire game was around 200 lines. We now want to make the game more interesting by adding sound and graphics. We also want to support mobile users. Because our time is precious to us, we don't want to reinvent the wheel. We will use a game engine to do the low-level heavy lifting for us, but before doing that, we need to step back and look at a more formal approach to our development. This chapter presents some development and design theory. Our Pong game will receive its game engine in the next chapter.

2.1 Development Strategies

2.1.1 Progressive Enhancement and Graceful Degradation

Progressive Enhancement and Graceful Degradation are two strategies with the same goal of supporting as many devices as possible though they take opposite strategies.

Progressive Enhancement is the idea that you build your website to run on the weakest link possible. Perhaps you may not go as far back as IE6 (web developers like to keep their sanity), but turning off JavaScript on your browser as you build the site could be considered part of this strategy.

The core goal is to build your site using nothing but well-established standards and HTML tags focused on the meaning of the content rather than presentation (such as using <cite> to cite a reference versus <i> to just italicize it).

After your site is built this way, if a newer more capable browser comes along, you can add hooks to your solid foundation of code to give the user a better experience.

Graceful Degradation takes the opposite approach. It is the idea that you want to give your users the best experience possible. If they have a highly capable device, you want to give them the means to use it.

If a less-capable browser comes along, you want the code to "gracefully degrade." For example, if the user does not have JavaScript enabled, instead of serving a broken page, you make sure your site was written in a way that still renders something workable to that user. Maybe not all features are available, but the core content is still accessible.

The pong game we have been developing does a poor job of graceful degradation. A browser without Canvas support will just get a blank or broken page. This is not acceptable in professional development. Many game engines (such as Crafty) support DOM-based drawing versus using pure Canvas. In the games you develop yourself, you should experiment with both and see which has the best performance on the browsers you want to support.

There are pros and cons to each strategy, and the proper approach could be the topic of a nice debate. The best strategy is dependent on the task. For example, a very content-oriented website (such as Wikipedia) benefits greatly with a progressive enhancement approach.

Video game development benefits from a graceful degradation approach. Audio is a big problem with HTML5 and mobile devices. The standard approach is to just turn sound off for mobile devices accessing via their internal browser. That doesn't mean our app should be built without sound and then bolted on later. Eventually, mobile HTML5 audio will improve, the users will upgrade their phones, and our game will be ready for them.

There is a third, hybrid strategy to consider when developing a game or any app. It is called "mobile-focused development." This strategy is also known as "Mobile First" and is often discussed when discussing the term *responsive design*. The idea is that mobile devices present a very unique challenge, and to give them a good experience, their needs must be addressed from Day 1. This strategy warrants an entire section. We intend to support mobile devices in this book.

2.1.2 Mobile-Focused Development

Developers love their mice and keyboards. It makes for fast and precise work. However, once your app leaves your workstation, chances are a mobile user will try to access it. If your app won't run on their device, they will leave and possibly not come back. Depending on the stat agency and how the metric is calculated, mobile web access via tablets or phones now accounts for anywhere from 13% [36] to 27% [37] of all internet usage, and that number will continue to rise quickly as smartphones for the first time outsold "dumbphones" in 2013 [38].

If you don't focus on mobile web users, your audience will shrink. Even users that are usually on a desktop browser very likely have a mobile internet device as their secondary. Naturally, they would prefer that your app worked on both.

There is actually a side benefit to such focus on mobile users: Their devices are weak. The current generation (mid-2013) high-end cell phones and tablets boast a power-conserving 1.4 GHz dual-core processor and usually 1 GB of RAM. The graphics processing unit is often embedded in the CPU. To find a current desktop with specifications that weak, you would have to reach for the low end of the all-in-one Black Friday deals. We as developers have been spoiled with multicore processors, lots of RAM, and good graphics processing being standard issue since 2008. Targeting mobile devices forces us to keep our apps fast and efficient. If your app can run tolerably on weak mobile devices at varying resolutions, it will probably run smoothly on a desktop.

Notice I didn't mention our "big monitors" or "nice display resolution" in that paragraph about developers being spoiled by their workstations. This is because the monitor market has seen little innovation since 2006. This is because TV manufacturers tend to focus on just one market: HDTVs. That means computer monitor resolutions have been frozen at 1080p (1920 × 1080 pixels) for several years. Current tablets already exceed this resolution (iPad has 2048 × 1536) [32] while phones are just now meeting it (Samsung Galaxy S4 is 1920 × 1080 [39]).

An interesting situation has occurred with the fast improvement of mobile devices and stagnation of computer monitors: By the time you read this book, it is quite possible your 5-inch cell phone will be able to play your game at a higher resolution than your desktop. This is already true for many tablets.

2.2   Browser Wars?

Web developers are familiar with fighting all the different web browsers and keeping track of who is in the lead, a fight often called "The Browser Wars." However, once you dig deeper and factor in mobile, you will see that this war is long over.

2.2.1   WebKit/Blink

On the desktop, there are several browsers with various shares of the market.
They range from 10% to around 30% with Chrome as the market leader. There
is no real market domination on the desktop, but it is possible Chrome may
break away further and achieve a significant lead by the time you read this
book. Chrome had a strong upswing in 2012–2013 gaining 8% [40]. See the
chart in Figure 2.1. Note that Opera was left out since it only has 1% on the
desktop.

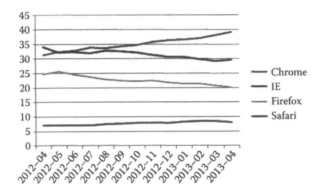

Figure 2.1. Desktop browser share April 2012–April 2013.

However, as web developers, the name on the browser does not matter
so much. It is the actual underlying engine, how the browser processes our
HTML5, that we are concerned about. See the next chart in Figure 2.2 of
market share with the common engines combined.

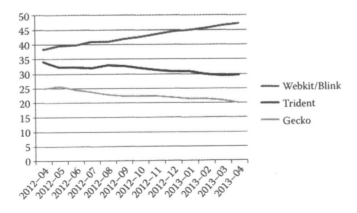

Figure 2.2. Desktop browser engine share April 2012–April 2013.

Webkit/Blink controls almost half of the desktop browser market. On April 3, 2013, Google forked the Webkit project and called it Blink [45], and as of version 28, Google is now deploying Blink as the rendering engine that powers Chrome [104]. The two will certainly diverge (e.g., Blink will not support any new vendor-specific CSS prefixes [44] (e.g., "-webkit-transform"), and Blink may abandon support for CSS Regions [66]), but for now, they are similar enough to be grouped together.

On mobile, the story on the surface looks about the same, with a handful of big players but no significant winner. See Figure 2.3.

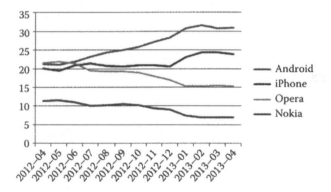

Figure 2.3. Mobile browser market share April 2012–April 2013.

Now, the same as before, the combined chart showing only the engines powering the browser. See Figure 2.4.

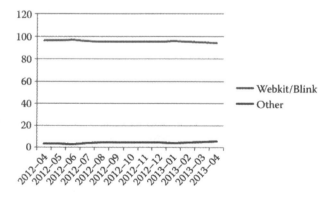

Figure 2.4. Mobile browser engine share April 2012–April 2013.

In the mobile landscape, there is essentially only one engine: WebKit/Blink. The two mobile market leaders (iOS and Android) both use WebKit/Blink as their base rendering engine, and the next closet leader, Opera, has announced a migration to Blink [41] (as it follows the Chromium project with Google).

This means the odd discrepancy when testing against multiple browsers may happen less often. However, iOS and Android web page behavior are not completely identical. Apple's Safari uses Webkit's built-in JavaScriptCore for their JavaScript engine, while Google's Chromium project uses the V8 JavaScript engine for theirs [43]. Still, unlike desktop development, if you get it working on one, you are very close to getting it to work on the other.

Since Chrome is available on both Mac and Windows and uses the Webkit/Blink engine, and since it is also has best-in-class web development tools built in, it should be your browser of choice for mobile-focused development. If you are a fan of Firefox, it too has really good developer tools (launch using Ctrl+i, same as Chrome). Still, keep Chrome around because you need a WebKit-derived browser to support your testing. If you are a Windows user, you have little choice because Apple abandoned Safari for Windows as of Safari 6 [31]. Opera's Blink-based browser was still in beta as of this writing.

2.2.2   Opera Mobile, Firefox Mobile, Windows Phone 8

All of the browsers in this subsection can be considered footnotes in development support. They are all very capable browsers, but they have not gained significant market share, and some of that can be attributed to Apple's policy of not allowing any of these competing browsers into the iTunes store (clause 2.17 states browsers must use iOS Webkit [46]). The iTunes ban immediately eliminates 25% of the mobile browser competition. Essentially, we are only discussing alternative browsers available for Android when we discuss non-Webkit mobile browsers. This market is extremely small.

Opera was an early entry in mobile browsing. They developed an innovative feature with Opera Mini where they would perform server-side processing and send a low bandwidth result to the mobile device. This is exceptionally useful in cases where bandwidth is sparse or expensive (or both). Because of this unique feature, Opera Mini was allowed in iTunes. Opera was also one of the first mobile browsers that rendered pages well. These two features made Opera very dominant in mobile. Currently, Opera still holds around 15% market share with strong popularity on Blackberry devices. While Opera Mobile has excellent HTML5 support, Opera Mini has weak HTML5 support. As mentioned earlier, Opera Mobile is going to eventually follow the Chromium project and use Blink as the rendering engine. As of early 2014, there currently has been no announcement if Opera Mini will follow.

Firefox's story is well-known. Firefox's meteoric rise on the desktop forced Microsoft to restart development on IE 6 after letting it stagnate for five years [47]. Firefox Mobile has good HTML5 support on Android. Despite its good performance, Firefox may not experience strong growth on Android because Android devices already come with a good built-in browser.

Windows Phone 8 users have Internet Explorer 10 as their built-in browser [48]. It has good HTML5 support. Currently, mobile browsing with Internet Explorer is hovering at around 1%. Microsoft has made a big push for mobile with Windows 8 and their Surface tablet. We can wait and see if mobile IE can compete with Webkit/Blink dominance.

2.2.3 Browser Detection versus Feature Detection

The old way of handling different browsers is detecting which browser is being used. Depending on how the browser identifies itself (by looking at the User–Agent string), you would serve up a custom-made page. This worked fine in the days of Firefox versus Internet Explorer. However, there are now far more browsers on far more devices and these browsers are updated very rapidly. In 2010, Google adopted an aggressive six-week release cycle for Chrome [49]. In 2011, Mozilla adopted a similar six-week major release cycle for Firefox [27]. Once you factor in all the mobile devices and the fairly large fragmentation of Android, you can see that sending up a custom sheet for each combination of OS + Browser is unmaintainable.

2.2.4 The Old Wrong Way

See Listings 2.1 and 2.2 for various methods of browser detection. One uses conditional comments inside HTML. Conditional comments are only supported in IE. Therefore, you may see the jQuery version of detecting the browser agent. **You should not do this**. It is presented below so you can recognize it because the technique has been very prevalent. Note that even jQuery does not recommend using it and has removed this feature as of version 1.9. Browser detection should only be a technique of last resort. IE10 does not support conditional comments [53].

```
<!-- Do not do this! -->

[if lt IE 7]> <link href="ie_6_and_below.css"
   rel="stylesheet" type="text/css">
<!--[if IE 7]>
 <link rel='stylesheet' href='ie7.css' type='text/css'/>
<![endif]-->
<!--[if IE 8]>
 <link rel='stylesheet' href='ie8.css' type='text/css'/>
<![endif]-->
```

Listing 2.1. IE conditional comments.

```
// Do not do this!

if ($.browser.webkit) {
  alert( "This is Chrome or Safari!" );
  //Do something just for WebKit
}
if ($.browser.mozilla) {
  alert( "this is Firefox!" );
  //Do something just for Firefox
}
if ($.browser.msie) {
  alert( "this is IE!" );
  //Do something just for IE
}
```

Listing 2.2. jQuery browser detect.

2.2.5   The Correct Way

The best way to determine if HTML5 features, such as Canvas, can be used on a browser is to simply ask or test if the browser supports it. If it does, then continue loading that branch of your app. For example, using the Modernizr library, a common test for HTML5 features is shown in Listing 2.3.

```
if(Modernizr.canvas && Modernizr.canvastext) {
  // Continue loading canvas
  if(Modernizr.audio) {
    // Which audio format to use?
    if (Modernizr.audio.wav) {
      //Use wav
    }
    if (Modernizr.audio.mp3) {
      //Use mp3
    }
    if (Modernizr.audio.ogg) {
      //Use ogg
    }
    //No audio format worked? Perhaps use no audio.
  } else {
    // Audio not supported. Perhaps use the old <embed> method.
  }
} else {
  // Degrade gracefully. Perhaps use DOM or check for Flash?
}
```

Listing 2.3. Feature detect with Modernizr.

Modernizr has dozens of different browser checks delivered in a small package. It uses lots of tricks and even tries to work around known "false positives," places where the browser says it supports a feature but further testing showed support is inadequate.

If you only care about a handful of these checks, the Modernizr website has a utility that can build a special version with just the checks you need. There is no configuration for Modernizr. Just include the JavaScript library, and it will generate a global "Modernizr" object that holds the results. Using feature detection with Modernizr allows anybody to use any browser they wish. If it happens to support Canvas, you can send them Canvas. If it doesn't, you can try to degrade gracefully.

2.3   HTML5 Sound and Music

Audio has finally risen to prominence with HTML5. It now part of the core specification with the <audio> tag. With it, you can create an in-browser player with controls with a single line. All previous methods to put audio inside a page required embedding Flash, QuickTime, VLC, or whatever the client happened to have installed monitoring for an embedded object. Despite this new specification, sound and music right now still have some rough issues.

2.3.1   HTML5 Audio Formats

Despite audio becoming a first-class citizen, none of the browser manufacturers were able to agree on a standard format for it. Through these disagreements, two dominant formats arose: MP3 and Ogg Vorbis. To create a proper audio player that can play on all major browsers, you need to include both formats and then let the browser decide which one to use. In the next four figures, all the major browsers are shown attempting to play a 5s Wav, 10s MP3, and 15s Ogg. Take a look at images in Figures 2.5, 2.6, 2.7, 2.8, and 2.9.

Figure 2.5. HTML5 audio test IE.

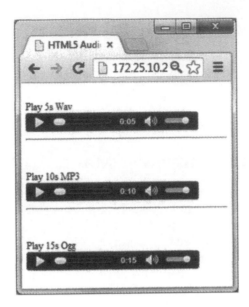

Figure 2.6. HTML5 audio test Chrome.

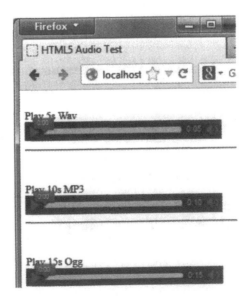

Figure 2.7. HTML5 audio test Firefox 21 Windows.

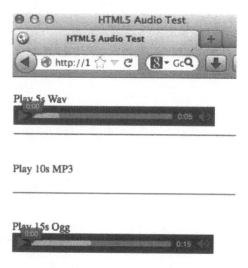

Figure 2.8. HTML5 audio test Firefox 21 Mac.

Figure 2.9. HTML5 audio test Safari.

The images are showing four browsers with three common formats, and results vary by platform and browser. IE only plays MP3. Chrome plays them all. Firefox 21 will only play MP3 for Windows. Safari does not play Wav. See Table 2.1 for a summary. Note that this chart may change by the time you read this book. While writing this book, Firefox 21 received MP3 support on Windows, and then Firefox 26 received it for the Mac.

Table 2.1. HTML5 audio codec support.

Browser	Ogg Vorbis	MP3	WAV
Firefox 26	Yes	Yes	Yes
Chrome 32	Yes	Yes	Yes
Safari 7		Yes	Yes
Opera 19	Yes		Yes
IE 11		Yes	

The only way to support all major browsers is to encode your files to MP3 plus Wav or Ogg. Since Ogg is significantly smaller than a standard Wav, that should be the preferred secondary format. Unlike MP3, Ogg is completely royalty free [50] [51], so it may eventually catch on to be a universal format for compressed audio.

Despite the annoying audio format war, previous problems of HTML5 are waning. With iOS 5 and below, you only had one audio channel to work with. Having one audio channel meant only one sound could play at a time. Audio hasn't been this crippled since the 1980s. Though the quality of the sound was very limited, the original 8-bit Nintendo supported five audio channels [52].

Though the problem is now solved in hardware by adding more channels, the original software workaround was to have "sound sprites" similar to a normal sprite sheet (discussed next chapter). You would have one big file with all your sounds. When an event occurred, you'd jump the audio player to the correct sound location, play the sound, and then jump the audio player back. It was crude, but it worked. Fortunately, iOS6 and recent Android has better multiple audio channel support. By the time you read this book, you won't need to worry about this, but keep that technique in mind if you want to support older browsers or old hardware (or simply enjoy game dev trivia).

To stay up to date on mobile and desktop browsers and what features of HTML5 are supported, you can visit http://html5test.com/. http://mobilehtml5.org is also a good resource for details specific to mobile.

2.4   Testing on Mobile Devices

Testing on desktop is pretty easy. Just open the HTML file, and see how it works. Tweak some code. Hit refresh. Mobile devices are not so simple because you are not directly editing your game on them (though you probably could, it would be very inefficient). Also, editing via the "File://" protocol does not usually work as it has lots of strict restrictions to prevent cross-site scripting and other security issues. In short, any serious website development needs an actual web server. This quick guide will teach you how to set up a local web server and connect your mobile device to it.

2.4.1   WAMP/XAMPP for Windows

WAMP (http://www.wampserver.com/) (and to some extent, XAMPP (http://www.apachefriends.org/)) is one of the easiest ways to get a development web server on your Windows machine. Two things to make sure of:

1. Install it in a directory your user account has write access to, such as: c:\Users\YourAccountName\wamp

   In the past, the normal procedure was to install the server in a folder off the root directory. This cannot be done as easily since Vista/Windows 7/Windows 8 has stricter permissions for apps. There will be file access issues. Also, some versions of these Windows-based servers have problems with spaces in directory names.

2. If you have VMware installed (to test different operating systems), you may need to reconfigure SSL to run on a different port. One of VMware's services likes to use 443, the default SSL port. For XAMPP, edit: xampp\apache\conf\extra\httpd-ssl.conf

   Search, find, and then change 443 to something else, like 4430. Figure 2.10 shows the SSL port being used by VMware and then starting on a different port.

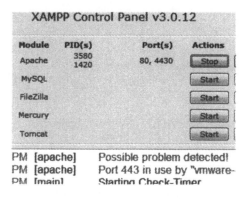

Figure 2.10. Starting XAMPP with VMware warning.

WAMP does not enable SSL by default, so port 443 will not be opened. If you are using SSL on WAMP, the location and file is very similar. Look for it at:

wamp\bin\apache\apache2.2.22\conf\original\extra\httpd-ssl.conf

Start WAMP/XAMPP and then start Apache web server. For this book, there is no need for MySQL or any other standard service beyond Apache provided by the web server. Go to http://localhost/ to verify that your web server is running.

If you are looking for a personal recommendation on which development server to use, I have used XAMPP for eight years. However, the project has been lacking since user account controls (UACs) became normal in Windows Vista, 7, and 8. As of this writing, the official instructions describe how to turn off UAC [89]. This is undesirable for a professional environment. For new development environments, I recommend installing WAMP. For Mac, I use MAMP. Apple's OS X Server's web server works fine too. MAMP is simply easier to configure and remap the web root.

With the web server configured, you now need to know your IP address so you can view your web page on your mobile device (on the local desktop, you can just use "localhost" or "127.0.0.1" as the web address). Follow these steps:

1. Windows Key + R, a command prompt appears.

2. Type "cmd". Press <enter>.

3. Type "ipconfig". Press <enter>.

4. Look for your IPv4 address. You may have more than one. Your web server will try to bind to all addresses.

See Figure 2.11 for an example IP address output. You can see my IP address is 192.168.1.23. If I had another adapter connected (such as Ethernet), it would show as connected too, and I would have another IP address. You may want to give yourself a static IP address because you will be frequently visiting this address on your mobile devices. Note that you can give a single network adapter multiple IP addresses. This can be useful for testing separate networks with a single adapter (often called a "network bridge"). Also, if you have VMware installed, you may have additional virtual adapters with additional IP addresses being shown as connected. Find the IP addresses of the adapter that is connected to your local network.

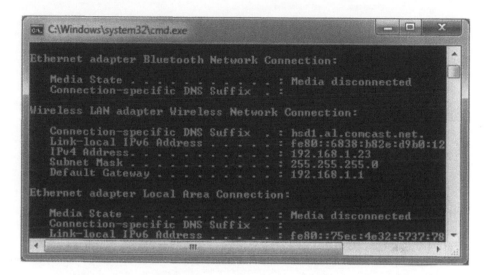

Figure 2.11. Windows 7 ipconfig.

Direct your mobile device's browser to each entry in your list of IPV4 addresses. One of them should show the default welcome page. If none work, check that your mobile device is connected to Wi-Fi and not 3G/4G. If Wi-Fi is connected, try turning off Windows firewall (but don't leave it off; set up a rule instead). Also, WAMP has two modes. Try clicking your WAMP task bar icon and select "Put Online." One of WAMP's modes is to just bind locally.

2.4.2 IIS for Windows

My personal recommendation for Windows web server development is WAMP presented earlier. I enjoy using the LAMP (**L**inux + **A**pache + **M**ySQL + **P**HP/**P**ython) stack, and WAMP quickly provides the "AMP" portion for Windows. However, Microsoft makes a capable web server available to Windows users. Setup requires a bit of effort. It involves navigating a lot of Control Panel options and advanced settings. The process is presented below. If you are happy with WAMP, then skip this section.

1. Press WinKey and search and launch "Programs and Features". Go to "Turn Windows Features on or off."

2. Check to turn on Internet Information Services. It will enable a lot of standard defaults.

3. **Important**: Navigate to "World Wide Web Services" → "Application Development Features" and enable CGI. This is needed for PHP, which will be installed later.

4. Click OK. When finished, go to http://localhost/ on your browser to see the IIS splash screen. With the web server working, you now need PHP (required for the Impact game engine).

5. Download and install the PHP plugin for IIS at http://php.iis.net/.

6. Navigate to the default IIS web root, which is "C:\inetpub\wwwroot." Right-click on "wwwroot". Select Properties.

7. We are going to enable our account to have full control of this directory. Select Security tab. Select Advanced. Select Change Permissions. Select "Add...." Type in your username. Click "Check Names." Click "OK." Give yourself full control. Click OK to dismiss the pop-ups cluttering the screen.

8. To make sure PHP is working, create a new file called "phpinfo.php" in your "wwwroot" directory. You should have write permissions to do this. Inside that file, put this:

```
<?php
phpinfo();
?>
```

9. To go http://localhost/phpinfo.php. You should now see the PHP information screen. This verifies IIS and PHP were installed correctly. The `phpinfo()` function can be used anywhere to check and verify PHP settings.

10. If you want IIS to load "index.php" by default, you can launch the IIS manager. (Press WinKey and search for "IIS manage"). Navigate to "Default Site." Look for "Default Document."

2.4.3 MAMP for Mac

Before diving into MAMP, the absolute easiest way to get a web server running on a Mac is to use Python's built-in HTTP server. Open Terminal (Go to Spotlight and search for "Terminal." It also can be found in Applications/Utilities). Navigate to the directory containing your web files. Now, run this command:

```
python -m SimpleHTTPServer
```

You will then have a very simple HTTP server running for that location on port 8000. Go to http://127.0.0.1:8000 to view your pages. The Python server will work for the majority of the examples. The main exception is the Impact game engine. Impact requires PHP. Eventually, you will need a web server with PHP support.

Now, on to MAMP. MAMP is the easiest full development server for Mac users. To install MAMP, download it (http://www.mamp.info/), unzip it, and then right click to open it. Note that you have to use right click because in OS X Mountain Lion and above, the GateKeeper feature prevents unsigned installers from running normally. Install with default options. Navigate to your Applications folder, and then run MAMP. If it all goes well, you will see Figure 2.12 after starting the app.

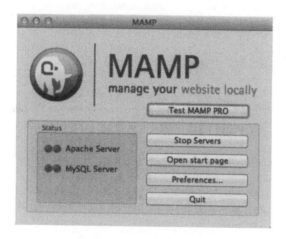

Figure 2.12. MAMP window.

We will not need MAMP Pro as PHP and Apache are sufficient for our purposes. Note: To ease development, you may want to set MAMP to use default HTTP port 80. Test the server by opening the start page. Now, you need to find the IP address of your Mac so you can go to it on you mobile device. To do this:

1. Start Terminal (Go to Spotlight and search for "Terminal." It also can be found in Applications/Utilities).

2. Type "ifconfig." Hit enter.

3. Look for your "inet" device. You may have more than one. As before, my IP address is 192.168.1.23. I use the same IP address whether in Mac or Windows to make my development easier (Figure 2.13).

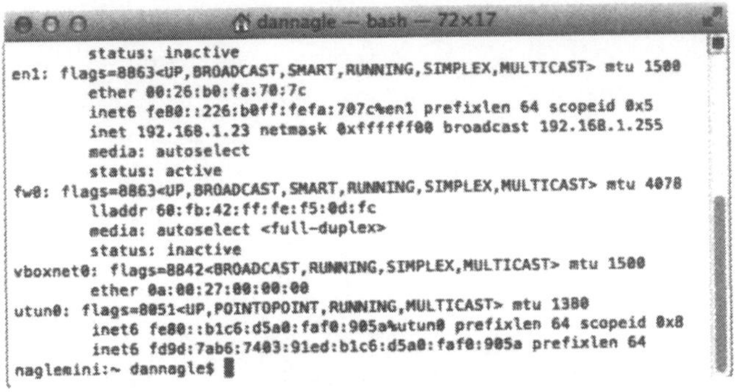

Figure 2.13. ifconfig Mac.

Navigate to that IP address on your mobile device. You should reach your Mac web server. With your IP addresses in hand, try each one on your mobile device to access the page. Make sure you are connected to Wi-Fi and not 3G/4G.

If you have access to a website with a web host, you also can upload and test your game in a private section of it. It's a bit slower than using a local server, but it is a lot easier to set up and share. Take a look at FileZilla in the Tools Appendix. Some programming editors, such as Komodo Edit, are capable of directing remote files through FTP and SFTP. That can save you the upload step.

2.5   Optimizing the Page for Mobile

Apple has developed specific meta tags to help optimize pages for mobile devices. Fortunately, instead of reinventing the wheel, Android and Firefox have adopted these tags. Unfortunately, IE seems to want to use its own extensions. IE-specific meta tags can be safely combined with Apple-specific meta tags. Web browsers will skip meta tags they do not understand.

The various techniques to get your site (and our Pong game) to work for mobile users will be discussed in this section.

2.5.1   Mobile Meta Tags

Mobile meta tags use meta, name and content in their tagging. The boilerplate for mobile devices is as follows:

```
<meta name="viewport"
      content="width=device-width, initial-scale=1.0">
<meta name="apple-mobile-web-app-capable" content="yes">
<meta name="MobileOptimized"
      content="width"> <!-- IE specific tag -->
```

These meta tags are telling the mobile device that the page has been optimized for mobile devices, and that it should set the viewport to the width of the device. There are many useful meta tags, such as setting the home screen button if the link is saved on an iPhone, but this is enough to get started. If you would like a shortcut to the proper ways of serving mobile and desktop users (and I am a big fan of shortcuts), HTML5 Boilerplate is an all-in-one starting template to build a modern HTML5-based website. It is discussed in the Tools Appendix.

2.6 Chrome Developer Tools

The Chrome Developer Tools are a very powerful set of tools for troubleshooting problems with your web page. To get to it, navigate to View → Tools → Developer Tools. You can also right click an element and "inspect" the element to launch the tools.

Despite the seemingly DOM-centric focus, there are a large number of useful features available to the HTML5 Canvas developer. Launch the Chrome Developer Tools and consider these tabs:

1. **Network** is invaluable when troubleshooting timing and AJAX requests to the server. Beyond that, looking at this page is also a very quick way to determine if an asset is not getting loaded because of 404/Not Found errors.

2. **Profiles** is the place to go for performance tuning. Often, 80% of the time is spent in just 20% of the code. Focusing on optimizing that 20% of the code will have the biggest payoffs. The 80/20 rule is often called the Pareto Principle [90]. It may not be obvious where the 20% is occurring. Start "Collect JavaScript CPU Profile." Play the problem/slow area in the game. Stop the Profile, and then take a look. Chrome will show which functions are consuming the most CPU time.

3. **Console** is incredibly useful. Drop "console.log()" all over the code to get debugging information. Chrome's console is capable of accepting full JavaScript objects. The prompt also can evaluate JavaScript expressions.

Strive to become very familiar with Chrome's Developer Tools. They are very useful.

2.7 Summary

This concludes Part I of the book. In the previous chapter, we built a proof-of-concept HTML5 game that can run on all modern (desktop) web browsers.

The game was built entirely on standards-based technologies, so it will continue to be playable, and maintainable, for years to come. The game itself is rather dull. We have hit around 200 lines of code, and we still need to add sprites, sound, and mobile support. Before attempting those new features, we took a step back and used this chapter to discuss some higher level considerations, such as the needs of mobile users, the main browsers, and other development strategies.

In Part II of the book, we will stop writing everything from scratch and use game engines to help us. First, we will refactor and finish our Pong game using the conveniently lightweight Crafty game engine. Then we will build another lightweight game using the nongame-oriented EaselJS, and then a complex game will be made with the heavier engine Impact. Finally, we build our last game using the WebGL-based Turbulenz 3D game engine.

Part II

HTML5 Game Engines

Chapter 3

Crafty

3.1 Source Code

All of the source code and examples are available at the website http://HTML5GameEnginesBook.com/. All the code, graphics, and sound are licensed free for personal and commercial use (MIT and CC-BY-3.0). Crafty is dual licensed MIT or GPL.

3.2 Introduction

Crafty is an open-source JavaScript game library developed by Louis Stowasser [54]. It renders to either Canvas or DOM. Its emphasis is on being lightweight and easy to use. For that reason, it is a good candidate to rewrite the Pong game from the previous chapters.

In this chapter, not only do we rewrite Pong, we will introduce a few more HTML5 considerations and best practices that are more fitting to be discussed here than in Part I.

3.3 Crafty Pong

Our previous Pong game was completed in just a few hundred lines. This time around, we want to have audio and graphics. Our new game will be called Crafty Pong. When finished, Crafty Pong will have a similar line count as before, but it will support far more features. The code itself also will look completely different, as it will have essentially been rewritten from scratch.

One problem with game engines is that they have their own way of doing things, which means very little code gets reused. Crafty is no exception. Therefore, it is important to find an engine that will do what you need. Otherwise, you may be abandoning a lot of code at failed attempts.

From Part I, our header needs to be modified to add the Crafty and Modernizr libraries. Modernizr provides HTML5 feature detection for us so our code works better across multiple browsers. Since we are moving our app to an external file, we also are going to make tweaks to the meta tags to tell our browser not to cache the files. See Listing 3.1 for these changes.

```
<head>
  <meta charset="UTF-8">
  <meta http-equiv="cache-control" content="max-age=0" />
  <meta http-equiv="cache-control" content="no-cache" />
  <meta http-equiv="expires" content="0" />
  <meta http-equiv="expires"
    content="Tue, 01 Jan 1980 1:00:00 GMT" />
  <meta http-equiv="pragma" content="no-cache" />

  <title>Crafty Pong</title>
  <script src="crafty_v0.5.3.js"></script>
  <!--
  For convenience, we could just link directly to
  http://craftyjs.com/release/0.5.3/crafty-min.js
  -->
  <script src="modernizr-v2.6.2-dev.js"></script>
```

Listing 3.1. Crafty Pong header.

Note that Crafty hosts minified versions of its library on its website that we could link directly. Also, note again, the absence of `type='text/javascript'`. This is no longer necessary with HTML5. Also, we are now adding no-cache clauses in our meta tags. This is very useful when working with graphics and external JavaScript files. On production servers, you would allow the browser to cache and instead use versioning. See below for example versioning of external JavaScript files.

```
<script src="crafty.js?v=0.5.3"></script>
<script src="modernizr.js?v=2.6.2"></script>
<script src="pong_crafty.js?v=1.0"></script>
```

When you release a new version, change the `v=` to the new version description, and the next time your user visits, the browser will fetch and cache the new file. You should use this technique for all external assets (.js, .css, images, etc).

If you are using a scripting engine, such as PHP, you can have the server do the versioning for you. Below is an example of how to do this:

```
<script src="app.js?v=<?php
   echo filemtime("app.js"); ?>></script>
 <link rel="stylesheet"
   href="style.css?v=<?php echo filemtime("style.css"); ?>">
</head>
<body>
 <img src="myimage.png?v=<?php
   echo filemtime("myimage.png"); ?>>
```

Now, PHP will append the file's modified time to the end of the v= parameter. A change in file modification will change the value for v. This will automatically force browsers to fetch new versions. This is very useful since browsers tend to cache aggressively.

If you are using a web server, such as XAMPP, WAMP, or MAMP mentioned in Part I, your server supports PHP. I recommend switching to the automatic versioning method now. Browsers will sometimes cache even if you try to tell them not to with no-cache headers. However, they always fetch when given new version numbers. A stale cache can cause lots of lost time during development.

3.3.1 Hello Crafty

Crafty was chosen at this point for revised Pong because it is the lightest of the engines, but all the engines being reviewed in Part II could easily implement this simple game. Crafty just happens to be a good candidate for this sort of quick task. We will need to refactor our code for the Crafty way of doing things. For now, let's initialize our Canvas and display some text. This verifies we are set up correctly. See Listing 3.2 for the code and Figure 3.1 for the output.

```
function onload() {
  if(Modernizr.canvas && Modernizr.canvastext) {
    Crafty.init(320, 480);
    Crafty.background('#dbdbdb');
    Crafty.e("HelloWord, Canvas, 2D, Text")
      .attr({ x: 20, y: 20, w: 100, h: 20})
      .text("Hello Crafty!");
  } else {
    var yes = confirm("Download a better browser?");
    if(yes)
    {
      window.location = "http://google.com/chrome";
    }
  }
}
```

Listing 3.2. Initialize Crafty

Figure 3.1. Hello Crafty Chrome.

When Crafty initializes, it creates an additional container element called cr-stage. If you wish to center and style your canvas game, add this to your style sheet:

```
#cr-stage {
    border:2px solid black;
    margin:5px auto;
    color:white;
}
```

We have Modernizr to check to see if the browser supports Canvas. Normal usage would have a graceful degradation, but for now, we are redirecting unsupported browsers to download Chrome.

For clarity, this is the last we will see of Modernizr in this book. Just assume all the remaining examples in this book have a check to see if Canvas is supported. The other Modernizr feature we may want to use, audio format detection, is already provided to us by the Crafty engine. All the engines in this book provide audio format detection.

We have verified proper setup, but before moving forward, a brief discussion of how Crafty is organized is needed. Crafty is divided into three main pieces:

Entity
> A crafty entity is an object that can be placed onto the screen and react to events. For those familiar with object-oriented programming, this can be thought of as a "class." Entities are declared using Crafty.e. In our pong game, the paddles, ball, and score are entities.

Components
> Entities are comprised of components. This can be thought of as methods and properties in object-oriented programming. In our pong game, our sprites and audio declarations are components that get attached to our

entities when we declare them. We also will use built in components such as `SpriteAnimation`, `Collision`, `Mouse`, and `Touch`.

Events

Components react to events. Some events are specially defined, such as the `Collision` component, which will make available an event called `onHit`. Some are built in to the entity system, such as the `EnterFrame` event when the game loop restarts.

The entity declaration when finished with the game ball will look like this:

```
Crafty.e("gameBall ,2D,Canvas ,Collision ,SpriteAnimation ,ball0")
```

`gameBall` is the name of the entity. It is actually an empty component used to reference this entity. The rest of the string tells Crafty to add support for `2D`, `Canvas`, `Collision`, `SpriteAnimation`, and `ball0`, which is a sprite sheet component that was declared earlier. This full entity declaration will be pieced together as we build Crafty Pong.

Also, Crafty supports chaining similar to jQuery. See below:

```
//jQuery chaining 2 commands
$('#foo').addClass('off').removeClass('on');
```

Throughout this example, chaining will be used to immediately modify properties directly after each other.

3.3.2   From HTML5 Pong to Crafty Pong

It is time to re-create the paddles and the ball. Beacause it is so easy to add with Crafty, we will go ahead and add the game loop and keyboard controls. Note that we do not specify FPS. This is all handled internally by Crafty using either `requestAnimationFrame()` or `setInterval()` depending what works best on the client's browser. See Listing 3.3 for this rewrite.

```
function onload() {
  var BACKGROUND_COLOR = '#dbdbdb';
  var PADDLE_WIDTH = 100;   var PADDLE_HEIGHT = 10;
  var PADDLE_COLOR = '#000000';   var BALL_COLOR = '#000000';
  var BALL_RADIUS = 10;

  Crafty.init(320, 480);
  Crafty.background(BACKGROUND_COLOR);

  Crafty.e("topPaddle, 2D, Canvas, Color")
    .attr({x: 100, y: 10,
       w: PADDLE_WIDTH, h: PADDLE_HEIGHT})
    .color(PADDLE_COLOR);

  Crafty.e("bottomPaddle, 2D, Canvas, Color, Multiway")
```

```
        .attr({x: 100, y: 460,
           w: PADDLE_WIDTH, h: PADDLE_HEIGHT})
        .color(PADDLE_COLOR)
        .multiway(4, { LEFT_ARROW: 180, RIGHT_ARROW: 0 });

   Crafty.e("gameBall, 2D, Canvas, Color, Collision")
            .attr({x: 40, y: 240, w: BALL_RADIUS, h: BALL_RADIUS})
            .color(BALL_COLOR);
}
```

Listing 3.3. Pong Game Board with Crafty.

For just 20 lines of code, we are now initializing a 2D canvas, starting the game loop, and we can already control the bottom paddle with arrow keys. Crafty is doing a lot of heavy lifting. However, there is one small problem, which you can see in Figure 3.2.

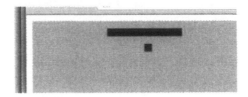

Figure 3.2. Pong Crafty square ball.

You will notice that the game ball is now a square. This is because Crafty does not support circles for entities. This is one of the downsides of game libraries; we can only do what the engine supports. That is, unless we wish to write extra code to extend the engine. We could do this since Crafty is open source [55]. What we will eventually do instead is use the Crafty sprite engine to load a round graphical ball. For now, a square is sufficient. Next, we need to add movement to the ball. This can be done by binding to the EnterFrame event. While we are at it, we will add hit detection to the ball. This is a lot easier with Crafty than it was with our old method. See below for the code:

```
Crafty.e("gameBall, 2D, Canvas, Color , Collision")
    .attr({x: 240, y: 240, w: BALL_RADIUS, h: BALL_RADIUS,
        xspeed: 2, yspeed: 3
        })
    .color(BALL_COLOR)
    .bind('EnterFrame', function () {

        this.x += this.xspeed;
        this.y += this.yspeed;

    })
    .onHit('bottomPaddle', function () {
        this.yspeed *= -1;
        this.y = 460 - BALL_RADIUS;
```

```
})
.onHit('topPaddle', function () {
  this.yspeed *= -1;
  this.y = 10+BALL_RADIUS;
});
```

Crafty lets us name entities, and then it uses its collision engine to see if the entities collide. This makes our job a lot easier. Notice we are using the same trick as before. We force the "y" value of the ball to something meaningful so it doesnt get "stuck" inside the paddle if a user slides into it. We almost have a working pong game. We now need to add a score. This requires a new entity with score variables. See below:

```
Crafty.e("scoreValue, 2D, Canvas, Text")
  .attr({x: 5, y: 12, w: PADDLE_WIDTH, h: PADDLE_HEIGHT,
    pointsPlayer:0, pointsComputer:0
    })
  .bind('EnterFrame', function () {
    this.text("You:" + this.pointsPlayer +
    "  CPU:" + this.pointsComputer);
});
```

The scores need to be updated. The code for this is not in a figure as it is simply incrementing the points variable when the ball leaves the stage. Next is the computer AI. It will be the same as before. The difference is that the AI is now inside the EnterFrame event of the top paddle. See below:

```
Crafty.e("topPaddle, 2D, Canvas, Color")
  .attr({x: 100, y: 10, w: PADDLE_WIDTH, h: PADDLE_HEIGHT})
  .color(PADDLE_COLOR)
  .bind('EnterFrame', function () {
    var gameBall = Crafty("gameBall"); //get gameBall
    if(gameBall.yspeed < 0)
    {
      if(gameBall.x < (this.x + PADDLE_WIDTH / 2))
      {
        this.x--;
      } else {
        this.x++;
      }
    }
    if(this.x <= 0)
    {
      this.x = 0;
    }
    if(this.x >= (320 - PADDLE_WIDTH))
    {
      this.x = 320 - PADDLE_WIDTH;
    }
});
```

Our last step is to prevent the user from scrolling the paddle off the screen. We need to modify the `EnterFrame` event of the bottom paddle. A pattern should be emerging. All the entities have an `EnterFrame` available to them that is convenient for adding logic. See below for the bottom paddle:

```
Crafty.e("bottomPaddle, 2D, Canvas, Color, Multiway")
    .attr({x: 100, y: 460, w: PADDLE_WIDTH, h: PADDLE_HEIGHT})
    .color(PADDLE_COLOR)
    .multiway(4, { LEFT_ARROW: 180, RIGHT_ARROW: 0 })
    .bind('EnterFrame', function () {
      if(this.x <= 0)
      {
        this.x = 0;
      }
      if(this.x >= (320 - PADDLE_WIDTH))
      {
        this.x = 320 - PADDLE_WIDTH;
      }
    });
```

We have now completely replicated the original HTML5 Pong game in Crafty (with the small exception of a square ball). We went from 230 lines to 120 lines. The use of the game engine also makes the code much easier to update, which we will demonstrate by adding graphics and sound.

3.4   HTML5 Game Graphics

Most games use a "sprite sheet." This is one big image containing lots of little images. To use a sprite sheet, you tell the game engine to load a single file, and then you tell it to display one small slice of the file. This is a very efficient way to handle graphics because the engine only has to perform one asset fetch (often a costly operation) and hold just one asset in memory. Also, since graphics are often repeated (particularly with overhead-style RPGs), having one image to rule them all saves memory overall. See Figure 3.3 for the sprite sheet used in our Crafty Pong game.

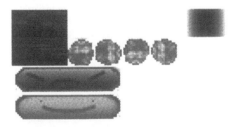

Figure 3.3. Crafty Pong sprites.

Writing a sprite sheet system for a game is difficult. You need to handle loading, unloading, and a coordinate system to slice up the image. Then you need to handle timed repetition if you want animation. Fortunately, we don't have to worry about that because all the game engines in this book have a sprite sheet engine. We just need to learn each system's way of managing it.

To use external assets in HTML5, such as a sprite sheet, you need to preload them. Browsers will happily show blank images if your game assets have not finished loading. A preload step makes sure the graphic is available in memory before applying it to the canvas. See Listing 3.4 for Crafty's loading and applying a sprite sheet.

```
Crafty.load(["pong_sprites.png"], function() {
    console.log("assets loaded");
    Crafty.scene("main"); //go to main scene
});

Crafty.sprite(16,"pong_sprites.png", {
    floor0: [0,0,1,1], //location=320,64, height=1, width=1
    floor1: [0,1,1,1],
    floor2: [1,1,1,1],
    wall1: [6,0,1,1],
    wall2: [7,0,1,1],
    ball0: [2,1,1,1],
    toppaddle:      [0,2,4,1],
    bottompaddle: [0,3,4,1]
});
```

Listing 3.4. Crafty preload sprite assign.

The load step tells the browser to fetch the sprite image. After it has fetched, it goes to the next scene, which is main. This strategy of having a load step before launching the game is used in every engine in this book (whether directly or indirectly via the way the engine is designed).

While assets are being fetched, Crafty reads the sprite declarations. The sprites ask for pixel size of each block, which is 16 pixels by 16 pixels for our purposes. Declaring them requires block coordinates, length, and height. If length or height is not specified, Crafty will set each value to 1.

We will now tile our background. Normally, if you have a complex map, you would have a tile map that goes along with your sprite map. You would parse the map and drop the tiles. Tile maps will be introduced with Impact (Chapter 5). For now, since this is just a one-level stage, we will hard-code the background tiles. See Listing 3.5 for code to draw the background.

```
Crafty.scene("main", function() {
  for(var ytile = 0; ytile < 32; ytile++) {
    for(var xtile = 0; xtile < 20; xtile++) {
        //console.log(xtile * 16, ytile * 16);
        var usefloor = (xtile%2);
        if(xtile % Math.round(Math.random()*10))
        {
          usefloor = 2;
        }
        if(xtile == 19)
        {
          Crafty.e("2D, Canvas, wall, wall1")
            .attr({x: xtile * 16, y: ytile * 16, z: -2});

        } else if(xtile == 0){
          Crafty.e("2D, Canvas, wall,  wall2")
              .attr({x: xtile * 16, y: ytile * 16, z: -2});

        } else {
          Crafty.e("2D, Canvas, floor"+usefloor)
              .attr({x: xtile * 16, y: ytile * 16, z: -2});
        }
      }
    }
```

Listing 3.5. Crafty draw background.

We are looping through and creating sprite entities throughout the background. The `floor+usefloor` portion decides which sprite to use. Just to make the background a little more interesting, a random sprite is thrown in. Also, when we are at the edge of the stage, we use a wall sprite. To make our paddles and ball use the new sprites, we need to modify their declarations. See below for their new entity declarations:

```
Crafty.e("topPaddle, 2D, Canvas, toppaddle")
    .attr({x: 100, y: 10, w: PADDLE_WIDTH, h: PADDLE_HEIGHT})
    //  .color(PADDLE_COLOR)


Crafty.e("bottomPaddle, 2D, Canvas,  Multiway, bottompaddle")
    .attr({x: 100, y: 460, w: PADDLE_WIDTH, h: PADDLE_HEIGHT})
    //  .color(PADDLE_COLOR)


Crafty.e("gameBall, 2D, Canvas, Collision, ball0")
    .attr({x: 300, y: 240, w: BALL_RADIUS, h: BALL_RADIUS,
        xspeed: 2, yspeed: 4
        })
    //.color(BALL_COLOR)
```

The new additions to our entity declarations are `toppaddle`, `bottompaddle`, and `gameball`. These were the sprites declared earlier. By adding them to our entities, our entities are now using sprite sheets.

Because we are using sprites, we removed the color component. We want our sprites to remain transparent. Because we are basing everything off powers of 2 (16 and 32 pixels), we need to go back and change the paddles and ball to fit. Crafty does automatic scaling, but the scaling looks bad without even sizes. We can see the tiled game in Figure 3.4, though it is not finished quite yet.

Figure 3.4. Crafty Pong tiled.

3.4.1 HTML5 Audio JavaScript

In the last chapter, we introduced the `<audio>` tag. HTML5 audio also can be controlled by JavaScript. This is crucial because we are no longer simply dropping an `<audio>` tag with multiple sources pointed to it. See Listing 3.6 on how to add our audio to the game. Crafty has the checks built in to correctly choose between mp3 and ogg.

```
//Add the files to the loader.
  Crafty.load(["spritesheet.png",
                "background_music.mp3", "background_music.ogg",
                "hit.mp3", "hit.ogg",
                "hit2.mp3","hit2.ogg"
                ], function() {
    console.log("assets loaded");
    Crafty.scene("main"); //go to main scene
});
  Crafty.scene("main", function() {

    Crafty.audio.add("backgroundmusic", [
      "background_music.mp3", "background_music.ogg"
      ]);
    Crafty.audio.add("hit", [
      "hit.mp3", "hit.ogg"
      ]);
    Crafty.audio.add("hit2", [
      "hit2.mp3", "hit2.ogg"
      ]);

    //-1 means loop background music forever.
    Crafty.audio.play("backgroundmusic", -1);
```

Listing 3.6. Crafty play audio.

Crafty lets you specify the number of repeats. If left off, it will play once. The "−1" means loop the sound forever. Those familiar with game design know the need of creating a nicely looping background song. When it gets to the end, it seamlessly transitions to the beginning. The user plays the game without noticing the restart transition. Unfortunately, an HTML5 audio loop is not seamless. There may be a slight pause as the game loops back to the beginning of the track. The break length may vary between browsers or even within restarts within the game. When designing HTML5 game music, make sure to account for a variable bit of silence at the end.

Now that we have added audio and graphics, we need to make the game mobile friendly. Crafty has built-in mouse events that double as touch events. To use them, we must bind our entities to them. The obvious first attempt is to add "Mouse" to the bottom paddle's Crafty constructor list and then bind to the click event. See below:

```
Crafty.e("bottomPaddle,2D,Canvas,Mouse,Multiway,bottompaddle")
...
.bind("Click", function(e)
{
    this.x = Crafty.mousePos.x;
});
```

The problem is that this event will only be active if the user clicks/taps on the actual paddle. We want the paddle to follow the user's finger even if it is not quite on the paddle. Crafty does not have a convenient global mouse binding mechanism. It only binds to entities. Therefore, to react to all mouse/touch events, we need to create a full Canvas-sized entity and bind the mouse to it. See below:

```
Crafty.e("mouseTracking, 2D, Mouse, Touch, Canvas")
    .attr({ w:320, h:480, x:0, y:0 })
    .bind("MouseMove", function(e)
    {
        //get bottomPaddle
        var bottomPaddle = Crafty("bottomPaddle");

        bottomPaddle.x = Crafty.mousePos.x - bottomPaddle.w/2;
    });
```

Our invisible mouseTracking entity takes up the entire screen and consumes the mouse and touch movements. It then fetches the bottom paddle entity and sets the X coordinate of the middle of the paddle to wherever the mouse/touch is.

This will react the same to both touch start and touch move since Crafty routes those events through the same code as its mouse events. This works well for our purposes, but keep in mind, touch is not the same as clicking. Mobile Safari has guidelines and rules regarding when it will send an actual "click." It involves the speed of the finger, the type of object being touched, the potential result, etc. [56]. In some cases, we will need to bind to touchstart and mousedown separately.

3.4.2   Sprite Animation

The last step is sprite animation. Sprite animation works by rapidly showing images with a slight variation to make it appear to move. As alluded to earlier, this would normally be a difficult task. Fortunately, adding sprite animation with Crafty is as easy as just declaring the entity supports sprite animation and what sprites to use. See the new declaration for our ball:

```
Crafty.e("gameBall,2D,Canvas,Collision,SpriteAnimation,ball0")
    .attr({x: 100, y: 100, w: BALL_RADIUS, h: BALL_RADIUS,
        xspeed: 2, yspeed: 4
        })
    .animate('BallBlinking', 2,1,4) //setup animation
    .animate('BallBlinking', 5, -1) //start animation
```

The first animate() command sets up the animation. It states where and the range of sprites to use. The next animate() starts the animation and says to loop it forever. What was once a black square at the start of the chapter is now an animated fireball.

3.5 Summary

We built a fully functional HTML5 game that can run on all modern web browsers and mobile devices, thus capable of reaching a very large number of users. Our game has sound, graphics, scoring, AI, keyboard controls, and touch controls. The game was built entirely on standards-based technologies, so it will continue to be playable, and maintainable, for years to come.

In Part II, we started off by building it from scratch, and then, in the first chapter of Part II we migrated to a game engine when we were ready for more heavy lifting. Crafty was chosen because it was lightweight and flexible, which is what we need for a quick game of Pong. There are many HTML5 game engines of varying strengths and weaknesses. Next, we will build a Tic-Tac-Toe game with the heavier EaselJS engine.

Chapter 4

EaselJS

4.1 Source Code

All of the source code and examples are available at the website http://HTML5GameEnginesBook.com/. All the code, graphics, and sound are licensed free for personal and commercial use (MIT and CC-BY-3.0). The CreateJS suite is MIT licensed.

4.2 Introduction

EaselJS is part of the broader CreateJS suite sponsored mostly by Adobe [58] and led by Grant Skinner [57]. Its goal is a suite of useful JavaScript libraries to build rich HTML5 applications. Much of its structure is Flash inspired. The CreateJS suite includes EaselJS, TweenJS, SoundJS, PreloadJS, and Zoe.

We are mostly interested in EaselJS., which is the portion that focuses on the Canvas element of HTML5. However, we will be using PreloadJS and SoundJS as well. Though video games may not be the original goal of EaselJS, in this chapter we will see it has all the necessary elements to build a respectable game.

4.3 Tic-Tac-Toe

Here is the problem statement for this chapter:

> "We want a 1-player Tic-Tac-Toe game written in HTML5 that demonstrates some of the abilities of EaselJS."

Despite being a very basic game, there is plenty of material to make a worthy tutorial with Tic-Tac-Toe. In this chapter, we will learn how to use EaselJS/CreateJS to preload assets, set up a sprite sheet, interact with mouse movements, draw shapes (the "O"), have collision detection, and play sounds. By the time we are done, we will have a good foundation to build more complex games with EaselJS.

4.4   Setup

CreateJS hosts minified versions of all its JavaScript libraries on their Content Delivery Network at http://code.createjs.com/. CreateJS allows direct linking of these minified libraries. For convenience, the example game in this book uses the all-in-one version of the CreateJS suite. See Listing 4.1 for the complete EaselJS header. Once again, your version should use versioning, preferably dynamic versioning.

```
<!DOCTYPE html>
<html lang="en">
<head>
  <meta charset="UTF-8">
  <title>Tic Tac Toe with EaselJS</title>
  <script src="createjs-2013.05.14.min.js"></script>
  <!--
  We could instead link directly to
    http://code.createjs.com/createjs-2013.05.14.min.js

  -->
  <script  src="tictactoe_easeljs.js"></script>
</head>
<body onload="onload()">
  <canvas id="canvas" width="600" height="600"></canvas>
</body>
</html>
```

Listing 4.1. EaselJS Tic-Tac-Toe header.

4.5   Hello EaselJS

With the header set up, we now need to test to see that EaselJS is working. For a minimal Hello World example, see the `onload()` function below:

```
function onload() {
    var canvas = document.getElementById("canvas");
    var stage = new createjs.Stage(canvas);

    var helloworld = new createjs.Text('Hello EaselJS!',
```

```
    'Bold 15px Arial', '#000000');

helloworld.x = 50;
helloworld.y = 10;

stage.addChild(helloworld);
stage.update();
}
```

The output is in Figure 4.1. EaselJS uses the concept of a stage with objects that are then put on the stage. After everything is set up the way you want, call update() to show the result. Flash developers will recognize some of the concepts of EaselJS because much of it was Flash-inspired.

Figure 4.1. Hello EaselJS Chrome.

4.6 PreloadJS for EaselJS

Just like when using Crafty, we need to preload our assets so we don't see blank images in our game. The CreateJS suite has a preloading library to make sure everything is ready. It is a little different than Crafty's version. First you need to set up a manifest object that will be passed to the preload engine, then you add function calls to the load events. Finally, call loadManifest(theManifest). See Listing 4.2.

```
function onload() {

    var manifest = [
        {src:"tictactoeboard.png", id:"tictactoeboard"},
        {id:"win", src:"win.mp3|win.ogg"},
        {id:"lose", src:"lose.mp3|lose.ogg}
    ];

    var loader = new createjs.LoadQueue(false);
    loader.onFileLoad = handleFileLoad;
    loader.onComplete = handleComplete;
    loader.loadManifest(manifest);
```

```
function handleFileLoad(event) {
        console.log(event.item);
}

//all assets loaded
function handleComplete()    {
    console.log("done");
}
```

Listing 4.2. EaselJS preload manifest.

The various events we are interested in are `onFileLoad` and `onComplete`.
`onFileLoad` gets called on each individual item, where `onComplete` is when everything is finished, and we can start the game. Our game will be launched
in `handleComplete`. However, we are not quite there yet. We have our images
loaded, but we still need to set up the sprite sheets and sound objects.

4.7   EaselJS Sprites

EaselJS supports a deep sprite sheet system. It has a large number of parameters, such as speed, frequency, chaining next animations, and more. To
use it, you declare a JavaScript object with all of these various parameters
for the sprite sheet. Our Tic-Tac-Toe does not have animated sprites, but, as
an example, see Listing 4.3 on how a sprite sheet may be loaded. This is the
bare minimum boilerplate with which to load an animated sprite sheet with
EaselJS. It is worth having here as a reference because it is tricky to set up.

```
var playerSpriteSheet ={
    "animations":
        {
        idle: [0],
        rolling: [0,1],
        flying: [12, 13],
        dying: [24, 27],
        idleflip: [11, 11],
        rollingflip: [10, 11],
        flyingflip: [22, 23],
        dyingflip: [24, 27]
        },
    "images": ["robot.png"],
    "frames":
        {
        "height": 16,
        "width": 16}
};
var playerss = new createjs.SpriteSheet(playerSpriteSheet);
```

Listing 4.3. EaselJS sprite sheet example.

The EaselJS sprite sheet system separates the images into frames based on the "frames" declaration. It starts at the top left, counting at zero, and then it reads left to right assigning each a number. The EaselJS documentation has a lot of detail about this. Sprite sheets also happen to be the easiest way to display a static image. Our Tic-Tac-Toe board is a one frame sprite sheet. See Listing 4.4 for the declaration and how to display the image. Note that our "frame" is the size of the entire image.

```
var tttSpriteSheet ={
    "animations":
        {
        idle: [0]
        },
    "images": ["tictactoeboard.png"],
    "frames":
        {
        "height": 600,
        "width": 600}
};
var tttss = new createjs.SpriteSheet(tttSpriteSheet);

var canvas = document.getElementById("canvas")
var stage = new createjs.Stage(canvas);

//all assets loaded
function handleComplete()
{

    console.log("done");
    var gameboardimage = new createjs.BitmapAnimation(tttss);
    gameboardimage.x = 0;
    gameboardimage.y = 0;
    gameboardimage.gotoAndPlay("idle");
    stage.addChild(gameboardimage);
    stage.update();
```

Listing 4.4. EaselJS Tic-Tac-Toe board.

A big cause of debugging frustration is simply forgetting to add the object to the stage. Equally frustrating is forgetting to call `update()`. EaselJS supports multiple stages and multiple canvases. They can all be juggled and managed independently. This can be very useful if your game needs to suspend one game to handle a side adventure.

See Figure 4.2 for our Tic-Tac-Toe game board being displayed.

Figure 4.2. Tic-Tac-Toe game board.

Audio in EaselJS is just as easy to use as it was for Crafty. The sound needs to be registered, and then it is easy to play. See below:

```
//only need to register once.
createjs.Sound.registerSound("win.mp3|win.ogg", "win");

//registered sounds can be played anytime.
createjs.Sound.play("win");
```

Like Crafty, EaselJS detects and plays the format compatible with the user's browser.

4.8 Tic-Tac-Toe Implementation

We have our images and audio loaded. We are ready to start the game logic. In our Crafty Pong game, we were very frame driven. In our EaselJS Tic-Tac-Toe game, we will be entirely event-driven. EaselJS allows easy binding to every frame, and that process will be shown for educational purposes, but our Tic-Tac-Toe game does not need it. Right now, we need to bind to mouse movements and touch events. Unlike Crafty, EaselJS supports canvas-wide mouse binding. We do not need to create a hidden entity. See Listing 4.5 for how to bind touch and mouse.

```
// enable touch interactions if supported on the device:
createjs.Touch.enable(stage);

stage.addEventListener("stagemousedown", mouseDownEvent);
stage.addEventListener("stagemouseup", mouseUpEvent);

  function mouseDownEvent(event) {

      console.log("mousedown/touchstart");
    stage.addEventListener("stagemousemove"
```

```
        , mouseMoveEvent);
    }

    function mouseUpEvent(event) {

        console.log("mouseup/touchend");
        stage.removeEventListener("stagemousemove"
            , mouseMoveEvent);
    }

    function mouseMoveEvent(event) {
        console.log("mousmove/touchmove");
    }
```

Listing 4.5. EaselJS bind to mouse/touch.

As mentioned before, mouse events do not always equal touch events, but like Crafty, EaselJS routes the touch logic through the mouse logic. To enable this path of logic, declare Touch to be enabled. If Touch is not declared to be enabled, the mouse will operate correctly, but when an iPad user attempts to use your game, Mobile Safari will interpret the finger swipe to be a page scroll instead of giving the event to your game.

With the code in Listing 4.5, our Chrome debugger console should be outputting debug data with every mouse event. We can see the user pressing the mouse button down, moving the mouse, and then lifting the mouse button. These are all the events needed for our game. See Figure 4.3 for the results of our tests.

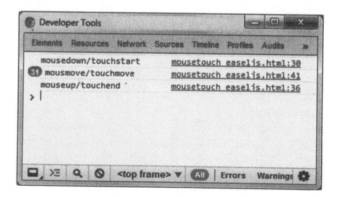

Figure 4.3. EaselJS touch mouse tests.

We can now start adding logic. We see the mouse/touch event occur, but we don't know which area of the game board the user wants the "X". To do this, we slice up our game board into the game areas for hit detection. See below:

```
var areaArray = Array(9);

for(var i=0;i<9;i++)
{
    areaArray[i] = Object();
    areaArray[i].diameter = 130;
    areaArray[i].value = "";
}

areaArray[0].x = 38; areaArray[0].y = 61;
areaArray[1].x = 228; areaArray[1].y = 61;
areaArray[2].x = 420; areaArray[2].y = 61;

areaArray[3].x = 38; areaArray[3].y = 227;
areaArray[4].x = 228; areaArray[4].y = 227;
areaArray[5].x = 420; areaArray[5].y = 227;

areaArray[6].x = 38; areaArray[6].y = 401;
areaArray[7].x = 228; areaArray[7].y = 401;
areaArray[8].x = 420; areaArray[8].y = 401;
```

We are slicing up our game board like an EaselJS spite sheet. These x and y values were determined through a little math plus experimentation. If there was a large number of squares in the game, then math would be used exclusively. However, with just nine squares, hard-coding values is sufficient. Most of this game will be hard-coded for simplicity.

Next, we need to add collision detection to the mouse move event. See Listing 4.6 for adding it to mouse move and Listing 4.7 for the actual collision detection function. This is a very important piece. It is the first time we needed to detect collision on all four sides.

```
function mouseMoveEvent(event)
{
  var newPoint = new Object();
  newPoint.x = stage.mouseX;
  newPoint.y = stage.mouseY;
  newPoint.diameter = 15;

    for(var i=0; i<areaArray.length; i++)
    {
        if(collisionDetect( areaArray[i], newPoint))
        {
            console.log("hit detect on", i);
            areaArray[i].value = "x";
            break;
        }
    }
}
```

Listing 4.6. Add hit detect to mouse move.

```
function collisionDetect(object1, object2)
{
    var ax1 = object1.x;
    var ay1 = object1.y;
    var ax2 = object1.x + object1.diameter;
    var ay2 = object1.y + object1.diameter;

    var bx1 = object2.x;
    var by1= object2.y;
    var bx2= bx1 + object2.diameter;
    var by2= by1 + object2.diameter;

    if (ax1 <= bx2 && ax2 >= bx1 &&
            ay1 <= by2 && ay2 >= by1)
    {
        return true;
    } else {

        return false;
    }

}
```

Listing 4.7. Basic collision detection.

What we are doing is looping through all the Tic-Tac-Toe areas and detecting if the mouse collided with that area. The collision detection function used in Listing 4.7 is the standard "bounding box" collision detection. All the pathways in the `if` statement must be true for one rectangle to have collided with another rectangle. To have adjacent items also be considered collided, modify the `if` statement by removing the `=`.

If the area has collided with the mouse, we save the object's value to "x" so it can be looked at later to determine computer movement and win conditions. The game now knows the state of the game board, but the player doesn't. We need to draw the "X". Note we are adding lots of unneeded complexity with our mouse tracking. This game would be far, far easier to implement if the user just clicked/touched the area for the desired placement of their "X" and then just have the "X" appear. There would be no mouse movement tracking required, but that wouldn't make a very interesting tutorial. The reason we want mouse/touch movement is because we are instead going to follow the mouse and actually paint the "X" as the player is drawing it. That's more interesting, and EaselJS has nice drawing libraries to help us.

To get started with drawing, we need a drawing canvas. We also need a player color and computer color. We need to prevent the player from drawing in more than one area. We need to update the stage. There is a lot more code to add. See Listing 4.8 for the changes. This completes the setup logic. The rest of the game will happen in mouse events.

```
var xoCanvas = new createjs.Shape();
stage.autoClear = false; //leave markings

var playerTurn = 2; //player gets 2 strokes
var hitdetected = false;
var gameOver = false;
var colorPlayer = "#75CAF4"; var colorComputer = "#49FF3F"
var previousPoint = new Object();
previousPoint.x = previousPoint.y = 0;

//all assets loaded
function handleComplete() {
    var gameboardimage = new createjs.BitmapAnimation(tttss);
    gameboardimage.x = 0;
    gameboardimage.y = 0;
    gameboardimage.gotoAndPlay("idle");
    stage.addChild(gameboardimage);

    stage.addChild(xoCanvas); // where the drawing happens.

    createjs.Sound.registerSound("bombboom.mp3|bombboom.ogg",
        "bombboom");
    createjs.Sound.registerSound("restart.mp3|restart.ogg",
        "restart");

    createjs.Ticker.setFPS(30);
    createjs.Ticker.addEventListener("tick", tick);

}
function tick() {
  stage.update();
}
```

Listing 4.8. More Tic-Tac-Toe setup.

Notice the addition of the `tick()` function. As promised, this is the EaselJS equivalent to Crafty's `EnterFrame` event. If some background logic is needed, it can go here. As all our events are mouse/touch driven, the only thing we are interested in is updating the stage. Now that you have seen how to do it, this tick event will be removed and the stage will be manually updated as needed. Also, notice `xoCanvas` has been added to the stage. This is being used as a container to hold all the X's and O's being drawn. When we draw, we will draw to this canvas. Adding this canvas to the stage draws all the X's and O's.

To mimic the user drawing, we will remember the previous point and then draw a line to the next point. It will happen as quickly as the `mousemove` / `touchmove` events fire. Although the underlying engine is drawing lines, to the user, it will look curved and follow their pointer. See Listing 4.9 for the code.

```
function mouseDownEvent(event) {
    stage.addEventListener("stagemousemove" , mouseMoveEvent);
}

function mouseUpEvent(event) {
    stage.removeEventListener("stagemousemove" , mouseMoveEvent);
    previousPoint.x = previousPoint.y = 0;
}
function mouseMoveEvent(event) {

    var newPoint = new Object();
    newPoint.x = stage.mouseX;
    newPoint.y = stage.mouseY;
    newPoint.diameter = 15;

    if(previousPoint.x > 0)
    {
    xoCanvas.graphics.clear().setStrokeStyle(newPoint.diameter,
     'round')
        .beginStroke(colorPlayer)
        .moveTo(newPoint.x, newPoint.y)
        .lineTo(previousPoint.x, previousPoint.y);
    }
    previousPoint.x = newPoint.x;
    previousPoint.y = newPoint.y;
```

Listing 4.9. Mouse draw events.

What is happening is as soon as touch/mousedown occurs, we start listening for movement. When the move event fires, we can draw a line from the previous point to the new point. setStrokeStyle() says to use a round pattern with a radius of 15. moveTo() moves the paintbrush to the mouse's X,Y. lineTo() draws the line to the previous point. When the mouseup/touchend event occurs, we stop looking for movement. We also set the previous point to 0 so we know not to look at it when we start again. This code is sufficient to draw an X. See Figure 4.4.

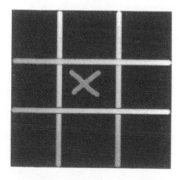

Figure 4.4. Draw an X.

The game also is tracking that the square has been hit. Unfortunately, the game does not restrict just 1 square per turn. We need to add the logic from the variables added back on in Listing 4.8. We need to restrict to just one square and two strokes and one turn before the computer can take over and set the variable flags back. See Listing 4.10 for the completed `mousemove` event handler.

```
function mouseMoveEvent(event) {
if(playerTurn)   {
  var newPoint = new Object();
  newPoint.x = stage.mouseX; newPoint.y = stage.mouseY;
  newPoint.diameter = 15;

  if(hitdetected && previousPoint.x > 0)   {
    xoCanvas.graphics.clear()
    .setStrokeStyle(newPoint.diameter, 'round')
    .beginStroke(colorPlayer)
    .moveTo(newPoint.x, newPoint.y)
    .lineTo(previousPoint.x, previousPoint.y);
  }

  previousPoint.x = newPoint.x;
  previousPoint.y = newPoint.y;

  //find area collisions
  for(var i=0; i<areaArray.length; i++)   {
    if(collisionDetect( areaArray[i], newPoint)
      && areaArray[i].value == ""
      && playerTurn == 2 && !hitdetected
      )
    {
      areaArray[i].value = "x";
      hitdetected  = true;
    }
  }
}
stage.update(); //update faster for smooth lines
}
```

Listing 4.10. Mouse draw events with turns.

Several pieces of logic have been added. Let's go through them. We are only drawing during the player's turn and a valid collision was detected. What makes a valid collision? A valid collision is when the player hits a square that has not yet been assigned. Also, the player can only have one valid collision per turn. The collision is detected on the first stroke. The player gets two strokes so they can complete their X.

At the end of `mouseup/touchend`, a check is made to see if the player has won. If not, it is the computer's turn. See Listing 4.11.

```
function mouseUpEvent(event) {
    stage.removeEventListener("stagemousemove" , mouseMoveEvent);
    previousPoint.x = previousPoint.y = 0;
    if(hitdetected)   {
        playerTurn--;
    }

    //player turn over
    if(!playerTurn)    {
        if(checkWin("x")) {
            console.log("player win");
            gameOver = true;

        } else {
            //did not win. Computer turn
            computerMove();
            if(checkWin("o"))
            {
                console.log("computer win");
                gameOver = true;
            }
        }
    }
}
```

Listing 4.11. Mouse up event.

Our computer's logic is presented below:

```
function computerMove()
{
    console.log("my turn...");
    playerTurn  =2;hitdetected  = false;
    for(var i=0; i<areaArray.length; i++)   {
        if(areaArray[i].value == "")   {
            console.log("I choose ", i);
            areaArray[i].value = "o";
            addOh(areaArray[i].x,areaArray[i].y);
            break;

        }
    }
}
```

Indeed, our computer player is very dumb. It just scans through and finds the first available board position and takes it. This needs to be improved.

Tic-Tac-Toe is a "solved" game. If both players are playing optimally, the game always ends in a tie. The perfect strategy will never lose. There are thousands of possible board movements, but a winning AI strategy needs only be concerned with about a handful of them. If you wanted a perfect player, consider this common strategy (note that while opening with the corner is better strategically, it is not necessary):

- Always take the win.

- Always take the block.

- Always take the middle.

- Note that the board has symmetry.

- Hard code the rest of the scenarios.

This will reduce the number of game layouts from a few thousand to a couple hundred (rotate the board to find a matching layout). How to program a perfect tic-tac-toe player is not covered in this book, but it is a useful exercise. The first three strategies are easy and will be implemented. See below for scanning for the win condition:

```
//check for a win
for(var i=0; i<areaArray.length; i++)
{
  if(areaArray[i].value == "")
  {
    areaArray[i].value = "o";
    if(checkWin("o", false))
    {
        areaArray[i].value = "o";
        console.log("Found a win at ", i);
        addOh(areaArray[i].x,areaArray[i].y);
        return;
    } else {
        areaArray[i].value = "";
    }
  }
}
```

We loop through to see if placing an O will create a win. If it doesn't, we undo what we just did. We have a `checkWin` function that will be presented later. Essentially, it looks to see if the passed character, an X or O, has won. The second parameter states whether to draw the winning line. Checking for a block is identical. Just swap an O with an X. Therefore, it is not shown. Taking the middle trivial:

```
if (areaArray[4].value == "")
{
    console.log("Taking middle block.", 4);
    areaArray[4].value = "o";
    addOh(areaArray[4].x,areaArray[4].y);
    return;
}
```

With a touch of AI, our computer player is now a lot smarter. It is not perfect, but at least the player will need to try to fool it. We now need to draw the O for the computer. See below:

```
function addOh(x,y)
{
    x += 50;y += 50; //move to center
    var circle = new createjs.Shape();
    circle.graphics.beginFill(colorComputer).drawCircle(x,y,50)
    .beginFill("#000000").drawCircle(x,y,50-15);
    stage.addChild(circle);
}
```

Take a look at addOh(). It is actually 2 circles. One is drawn with a radius of 50 in the color of colorComputer. The other is drawn with a radius of 35 in a black color. This gives it a donut hole.

Next, we need our checkWin() function. See Listing 4.12 for the code for this.

```
function check3(a,b,c, winChar, drawit)
{
    if(areaArray[a].value == winChar
        && areaArray[b].value == winChar
        && areaArray[c].value == winChar)
    {
        if (drawit) {
            drawWin(areaArray[a],areaArray[c]);
        }
        return true;
    }
    return false;
}
function checkWin(winChar, drawit)
{
    //8 possible wins
    //rows
    if(check3(0,1,2,winChar, drawit)){ return true; }
    if(check3(3,4,5,winChar, drawit)){ return true; }
    if(check3(6,7,8,winChar, drawit)){ return true; }

    //cols
    if(check3(0,3,6,winChar, drawit)){ return true; }
    if(check3(1,4,7,winChar, drawit)){ return true; }
    if(check3(2,5,8,winChar, drawit)){ return true; }

    //diagonals
    if(check3(0,4,8,winChar, drawit)){ return true; }
    if(check3(2,4,6,winChar, drawit)){ return true; }

    return false;
}
```

Listing 4.12. Tic-Tac-Toe win code.

A more elegant solution would be to apply some math, but this is not necessary for Tic-Tac-Toe. There are only eight possible win conditions. It is easier to just hard-code. The check3() function takes the three areas, looks to see if they match the winChar, and returns true if it does. The drawit gets passed to state whether to draw the winning line.

Finally, we need to draw the final slash to represent the win. See below:

```
function drawWin(a,b)
{
    var useColor = colorPlayer;
    if(a.value == "o")
    {
        useColor =colorComputer;
        createjs.Sound.play("lose");
    } else {
        createjs.Sound.play("win");
    }
    var s = new createjs.Shape();
    s.graphics.setStrokeStyle(16, "round", "round")
        .beginStroke(useColor)
            .moveTo(a.x,a.y).lineTo(b.x+b.diameter,b.y+b.diameter);
    stage.addChild(s);
}
```

drawWin() accepts two areaArray objects. It looks at one to see the winning value so it knows which color and sound to use. It starts at the top left of a and draws to the bottom right of b. This is an easy method to cover the win zones, but it gives the line a slant, but overall, it looks well enough for our purposes. See Figure 4.5 for our final Tic-Tac-Toe game.

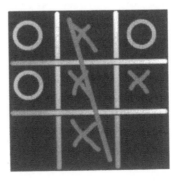

Figure 4.5. Tic-Tac-Toe win.

4.9   Summary

Though game development is not really its original focus, EaselJS, along with
the broader CreateJS suite, has all the tools needed to create a respectable
HTML5-based 2D game. Our entire game is only 400 lines, and we were able
to support both mobile and mouse, sound, preload images, add our own hit
detection, add computer logic, and ultimately win (or lose) the game. This
base could easily be expanded for a bigger game.

In the next chapter, we will build a new game with another engine. Impact
will be used to create MechaJet, a side-scrolling action, space-style, shooter
game that will introduce physics, tiles, and other concepts. Impact is the last
2D engine before diving into the very complex Turbulenz 3D game engine.

Chapter 5

Impact

5.1 Source Code

All of the source code and examples are available at the website http://HTML5GameEnginesBook.com/. All the code, graphics, and sound are licensed free for personal and commercial use (MIT and CC-BY-3.0). Impact is proprietary and is not distributed. It may be purchased at http://impactjs.com.

5.2 Introduction

Impact is an HTML5 JavaScript game engine developed by Dominic Szablewski [63]. It is the only proprietary game engine reviewed in this book. Despite its proprietary nature, the engine is delivered in source form so you can modify it. Also, the barrier to entry is (as of this writing) a modest, no-royalty, one-time $99 fee. You get a lot for $99:

Impact
> The engine itself.

Weltmeister
> A well-organized level editor with tight Impact integration.

Source code for Impact and Weltmeister
> Though these tools are not open source, you can still get benefits of low-level customization with access to the source code itself.

Demo games with source code
> The examples demonstrate collisions, scrolling, and physics.

5.3   Setup

Setup is a bit different from the other game engines. Though Impact development mostly works standalone, Weltmeister saving and loading requires the use of a web server with PHP. Also, the files in your project have to be structured a particular way. Once again, this is mostly to serve Weltmeister. If you do not care to use Weltmeister, you have much more flexibility. However, Weltmeister is a really nice tool, and adhering to its requirements is a small price to pay.

Publishing with Impact requires access to command-line PHP. This process, called *baking*, is a minify utility that combines all your files into a single .js file for distribution. You **must** bake your project before publishing. Otherwise, you may accidentally distribute the Impact source code.

5.3.1   PHP Web Server

See page 32 for details on how to set up a web server for development on a Mac or Windows. For the purposes of developing with Weltmeister and Impact, you can do everything you need by going to http://localhost/. To bake, you need the direct command-line path to php.

If you do not have the php command in your system path, you will need to know the direct file path. For Windows users with WAMP, php.exe is located at:
wamp\bin\php\php5.3.6\php.exe

For Windows users with XAMPP, php.exe is located at:
xampp\php\php.exe

For Windows users with IIS, php.exe is located at:
C:\ProgramFiles(x86)\PHP\v5.3\php.exe

Mac users with a web server probably have PHP in their system path. If you do not, MAMP puts the php executable at:
/Applications/MAMP/bin/php/php5.3.6/bin/php

Note that your version of PHP may be slightly different. Replace "php5.3.6" with the correct version. Take the full path you found and modify "bake.bat" for Windows and "bake.sh" for Mac to use it.

5.3.2   Impact Project Structure

Every project developed with Impact requires its own copy of the Impact and Weltmeister libraries in a folder accessible by your web server (Figure 5.1). In this chapter, we are developing the game MechaJet. Therefore, I have a folder called "mechajet_impact" as a subdirectory of my web server root at "www". Inside the project root there are a handful of files and directories. These serve a specific purpose.

Figure 5.1. Impact project file structure.

lib

This contains the core logic for Impact, Weltmeister, and your game. All your code will go into the "game" subdirectory inside this directory. All projects have their own copy of Impact and Weltmeister.

media

Graphics, tile sheets, audio, and other media go into this directory. This directory is by convention. The actual media files can be anywhere. You point to them when declaring your entities.

tools

The tools required to minify (bake) your project for publishing are found here.

dev.html

This is a file I created with the minimal required code to run and test the unbaked game.

weltmeister.html

Run this in your browser to launch the Weltmeister level editor.

index.html and game.min.js

game.min.js gets generated when you minimize/bake your project. index.html is identical to dev.html except inside the file it points to game.min.js instead of the unbaked project. index.html gets uploaded to the public-facing server, while dev.html stays local on the machine. Do not upload Impact itself to your web server.

Within the lib/game directory, there is another project structure governed by Impact and Weltmesiter.

entities

The core logic for your game objects are here. You will spend most of your time programming here.

levels

This holds your level files that are saved by Weltmeister.

main.js

The boilerplate start-up code that ultimately launches your first level goes here. This also contains your code that doesn't quite fit into a normal entity.

If you wish to change the arrangement of your files and have them still detectable by Weltmeister, there are some configuration options available inside lib/Weltmeister/config.js

5.4   Hello Impact

Impact is very easy to set up. When purchased, a link to download Impact will be emailed to you. Inside the zip package is a ready-to-go directory with all dependencies structured like mentioned above. Put the directory on your web server, go to index.html, and "It Works!" in Figure 5.2 is what you will see.

Figure 5.2. Impact Hello World.

Copy and paste the directory. Rename it to your game's name, then edit it directly as your starting point. This is the recommended way to develop with Impact.

5.5 MechaJet Implementation

In this chapter, we will create MechaJet, our example game for Impact. Here is the problem statement:

> "We want a 1-player action sidescroller written in HTML5 that demonstrates physics, tilesheets, animations, levels, and other abilities of Impact."

Impact is compact and well organized and, like before, little from the previous chapters will be reused in order to follow the Impact way of doing things.

To support both keyboard and touch controls in the sidescroller, "touch arrows" are being added. The best way to explain is to show the final screenshot. See Figure 5.3.

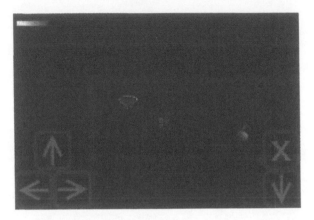

Figure 5.3. MechaJet screenshot.

5.5.1 Tile Map, Collision Map

In all the previous examples, we simply hard-coded the location of all our objects (particularly with our EaselJS Tic-Tac-Toe example). This is convenient for small games where tweaking values is not a big deal. However, our MechaJet game is going to be more complex. We want to have multiple levels (just two for this example), and we do not want to have to go through and tweak a lot of values to move an object around. Ideally, we would like to separate the level design from the game engine itself.

The answer to this problem is a "tile map". In our Crafty Pong game, we alluded to the use of a tile map. In this chapter, we will make a very simple one using Weltmeister. See Figure 5.4 for the tilesheet used in the map. Not shown is that most tile maps have an underlying collision map. Collision maps are the areas that are impenetrable from the user. Weltmeister solves this problem by having the collision layer have its own tiles that are drawn on top the tile map. This will be discussed later.

Figure 5.4. Tiles for MechaJet.

5.5.2 Entities

With Impact, every sprite that the player interacts with is an entity. In our game, we have four main entities with several subentities. The main entities are:

Player

The human-controlled player. The player can fly, run, get hurt, shoot, die, and respawn. Whenever the player shoots, it spawns another entity (PlayerBullet). For convenience, the bullet entity can be defined in the same file as player. However, only the root entity with the file named after it will appear in Weltmeister. See the sprite sheet in Figure 5.5. The sprites are tiny because Impact will be double-sizing everything. This helps performance. There is animation for rolling, flying, falling, and a death sequence.

Figure 5.5. MechaJet robot sprite sheet.

Buzzard

The buzzard flies back and forth, applies damage to the player, and dies in one hit. It also has a death sequence. See the sprite sheet in Figure 5.6. There is animation to fly and explode.

Figure 5.6. MechaJet buzzard sprite sheet.

Corridor

The corridor to the next level simply has a glow effect. Its sprite sheet is in Figure 5.7.

Figure 5.7. MechaJet corridor sprite sheet.

Bomb

Our bomb explodes when the player touches or shoots it. Instead of a sprite sheet, it is just a static image. It will be replaced with another static image when it explodes. These images are shown in Figure 5.8, and 5.9.

Figure 5.8. MechaJet bomb image.

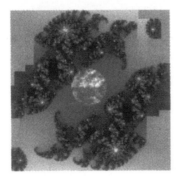

Figure 5.9. MechaJet bomb boom image.

What you don't see being defined above are the entities for our HUD (our "Heads-Up-Display," the health bar and arrow controls). Unfortunately, there is no convenient spot within Impact to put a HUD.

We could declare our health and arrows to be immortal entities with no gravity and hit detection. That is what we did with Crafty Pong, and that worked fine. Reusing that strategy *might* work here, but my experience has always found this path difficult. Impact and Weltmeister makes lots of assumptions for you, and if you aren't careful, your health bar may scroll off the screen along with your other entities. Instead, I have found the best way to do a HUD with Impact is to pull that logic out of the entities and directly apply the updates manually within the main game loop (defined in main.js). That way, we regain the control we need, and there is no chance Impact may misinterpret our intent with it. This technique will be shown later.

5.5.3 Buzzard Entity

We are finally ready for code. As mentioned before, you must write your entities in a certain way for them to work properly with Weltmeister, and we want to work with Weltmeister so our level design is significantly easier. This is an in-depth explanation of the buzzard entity broken into several parts because Impact is both dense and verbose. The examples following the buzzard will be a bit more high level. See Listing 5.1.

```
ig.module(
    'game.entities.buzzard'
)
.requires(
    'impact.entity'
)
.defines(function() {
EntityBuzzard = ig.Entity.extend({
    size: {x:16, y:16},
    gravityFactor: 0,
    collides: ig.Entity.COLLIDES.PASSIVE,
    type: ig.Entity.TYPE.B,
    checkAgainst: ig.Entity.TYPE.A,
```

Listing 5.1. Impact buzzard header.

Impact uses a file include structure that may have been inspired by Google Closure (for those who may have seen it). When you create an entity, you are actually creating a module that gets loaded into the Impact engine and Weltmeister. Wherever this entity is used, you must include the module in its ig.module list.

The module declaration is the file path minus the .js. The entity name is called Entity<Name Of Entity>. Both parts are capitalized. You can have other entities in the file, but the name of the core entity is the same as the file name.

That means our "buzzard" entity is declared as EntityBuzzard in a file located at game/entities/buzzard.js. This is the structure required to work with Weltmeister.

Inside the file, we have already declared some settings for our entity. Impact has lots of built-in parameters. Only a handful are actually required as it will make assumptions for whatever is missing. In our buzzard entity, we declared the size to 16 pixels by 16 pixels. The gravityFactor is 0 meaning Impact's gravity simulation has no effect on the buzzard.

Impact's built-in collision system is far smarter and more fluid than the crude method we used for EaselJS. It is actually a two-step system where it collides with the world and moving objects. Whereas our own collision system checked after we collided and then moved the object, Impact checks before it moves and has separate reactions depending on the collision settings. The different reactions are:

ACTIVE

An ACTIVE will collide with ACTIVE or PASSIVE and both will be separated after collision. Normally, players and enemies are declared PASSIVE. The buzzard is declared ACTIVE so it gets a bounce effect (determined by the "bounciness" variable) to look lightweight when colliding with a PASSIVE player. Separating the two also prevents the player from taking multiple hits.

PASSIVE

There is no separation when PASSIVE collides with PASSIVE. The units may walk through each other. The Bomb is declared PASSIVE so it does not slow down the PASSIVE player.

FIXED

Nothing will move this entity. This mode is used for the corridor.

LITE

Collides with ACTIVE and FIXED.

NEVER

Does not collide. The entity spawned by bomb explosion is declared NEVER.

The other portion of collision detection is declaring types. Friendlies should be declared `ig.Entity.TYPE.A` while baddies should be declared `ig.Entity.TYPE.B`. When an entity hits a type declared in its `checkAgainst`, that unit's `check()` function will be called. In there, the unit can give the other entity damage. See Listing 5.2 for the next round of code and explanation.

```
flip:false,
update: function() {

  if( this.vel.x == 0)
  {
    if(this.flip)
    {
    this.flip = false;
    this.vel.x = -10;
    } else {
    this.flip = true;
    this.vel.x = 10;
    }
  }

  if(this.vel.x < 0)
  {
```

```
        this.currentAnim.flip.x = false;
    } else {
        this.currentAnim.flip.x = true;
    }

    this.parent();
    },
```

Listing 5.2. Impact buzzard update.

At the top we have a new variable, called `flip`. This is used by us to track the direction of the entity. When the entity stops and we want to go in the opposite direction, we need to know the previous direction. This movement change decision happens in the `update()` function, which is Impact's way of processing code every frame. It is equivalent to Crafty's `EnterFrame` event and EaselJS's `createjs.Ticker.addEventListener('tick', myFunc)` function.

Our frame event tells the buzzard to move to and fro and change direction and spritesheet animation whenever it hits a wall. Impact is the first engine we have examined with a nice built-in physics system that saves us a lot of effort. Before, we were manually moving the sprites ourselves every frame. Now, we have a velocity variable exposed. We can give "vel.x" or "vel.y" as speed, and Impact will move the entity each frame for us. If we are traveling less than zero, we flip the sprite sheet over using `this.currentAnim`. Lastly, we don't bother looking or testing for collisions. We just look to see if we have stopped. If we have stopped, we can assume it is because the engine made us stop because we hit something.

The last piece calls `this.parent()`. Now that we've made our modifications, we pass control back to Impact. See Listing 5.3 for the rest of our buzzard entity.

```
    animSheet: new ig.AnimationSheet(
        'buzzardbaddie.png', 16, 16 ),

    check: function( other ) {
        other.receiveDamage( 20, this );
    },
    kill: function( ) {
        ig.game.spawnEntity( EntityBuzzardBoom,
            this.pos.x, this.pos.y);
        this.parent();
    },

    init: function( x, y, settings ) {
        this.parent( x, y, settings );
        this.addAnim( 'idle', 0.4, [0,1] );
        this.vel.x = -10;
    }
});
```

Listing 5.3. Impact buzzard init.

Impact's animation system slices a spritesheet from left to right labeling each image as 0, 1, 2, 3, etc. When it reaches the end of a row, it continues its numbering on the next row. To set up animation with Impact, give `AnimationSheet()` an image and the size of your sprites. For our buzzard, our sprite sheet image is "buzzardbaddie.png", and each section of our sprite sheet is 16 × 16 pixels. Inside the `init` function, we set up each animation. Our buzzard only has one animation, called `idle`. The delay between each frame is 0.4 seconds, and the frames used in the animation are located at 0 and 1.

Back to collisions. Earlier, we declared this entity to `checkAgainst` `ig.Entity.TYPE.A`. When it collides with type A, the `check()` function gets called. Here, we assign 20 damage to `other`, which would be the player.

The last piece is `kill`. Every entity has a `kill` function that gets called as it is being destroyed (similar to the idea of a "'destructor'" in object-oriented programming). For our buzzard example, we are going to spawn `EntityBuzzardBoom` at the current location. This is a small explosion effect/entity declared in the same file and presented in its entirety in Listing 5.4.

`spawnEntity()` is the preferred way to dynamically create entities within a game. Settings can be optionally overloaded by creating a settings object to be passed to the `spawnEntity()` function. The Player entity uses this to control bullet direction. Weltmeister also uses it to allow you to change settings on-the-fly within the editor, which will be demonstrated with the corridor later.

```
EntityBuzzardBoom = ig.Entity.extend({
  size: {x:16, y:16},
  collides: ig.Entity.COLLIDES.NONE,
  killTimer:null,
  animSheet: new ig.AnimationSheet( 'buzzardbaddie.png',
       16, 16 ),
  update: function() {
    this.parent();
    if( this.killTimer.delta() > 1 ) {
      this.kill();
    }
  },
  init: function( x, y, settings ) {
    this.parent( x, y, settings );
    this.killTimer = new ig.Timer();
    this.killTimer.reset();
    this.addAnim( 'idle', 0.5, [2,3] );
  }
});
```

Listing 5.4. Impact EntityBuzzardBoom.

The `BuzzardBoom` entity has no collision and uses the explosion animation section of our buzzardbaddie.png spritesheet. The notable edition `killTimer` has been added. Impact has a Timer object that is updated every frame to measure seconds of *game* time (not real time). Using the Impact Timer, the `BuzzardBoom` entity calls its own `kill()` function after appearing on the screen for 1 second. Note that because Impact adds default gravity, `BuzzardBoom` will "fall" out of the sky.

5.5.4 Bomb Entity

Our bomb entity is almost identical to the buzzard entity. It deals damage to the player when touched, and it explodes in its `kill()` event. The only subtle difference is that it doesn't move, it dies immediately when touched, and it plays a sound when it explodes. Listing 5.5 shows the complete bomb entity. Other than being slightly larger and using a different sprite sheet, `BombBoom` is identical to `BuzzardBoom`, so it is not shown.

```
EntityBomb = ig.Entity.extend({
  size: {x:16, y:16},
  collides: ig.Entity.COLLIDES.PASSIVE,
  type: ig.Entity.TYPE.B,
  checkAgainst: ig.Entity.TYPE.A,
  boomSound: new ig.Sound( 'bombboom.*' ),

  animSheet: new ig.AnimationSheet( 'bombitem.png', 16, 16 ),

  kill: function( ) {
    ig.game.spawnEntity( EntityBombBoom, this.pos.x-16,
      this.pos.y - 16);
    this.boomSound.play();
    this.parent();
  },

  check: function( other ) {
    other.receiveDamage( 50, this );
    this.kill();
  },

  init: function( x, y, settings ) {
    this.parent( x, y, settings );
    this.addAnim( 'idle', 1, [0] );
  }
});
```

Listing 5.5. Impact EntityBomb.

First, the collision type is PASSIVE so it doesn't slow down the player. Second, the `check()` function gives the player 50 damage and then calls `kill()` on itself. Like the buzzard, the kill function is overloaded. It spawns a no-collision "boom" entity called `EntityBombBoom`. Some offsets are applied because the bomb's boom is significantly larger than the bomb item. This puts the core of the explosion in the center.

Like all the previous engines, Impact will load the appropriate audio (.ogg or .mp3) depending on the browser's capabilities. This is performed with declaring the audio bombboom.*. The correct file is played whenever play() is called.

5.5.5 Corridor Entity

The corridor is an immortal fixed entity that looks to see if it has collided with the player. This creates a simple file with the interesting portion shown in Listing 5.6.

```
collides: ig.Entity.COLLIDES.FIXED,
type: ig.Entity.TYPE.B,
tolevel: "Mechajetlevel2",
checkAgainst: ig.Entity.TYPE.A,
health:9999,
check: function(other) {
  if (other instanceof EntityPlayer)
  {
    ig.game.loadLevelDeferred(ig.global["Level" +
                this.tolevel]);
  }
},
receiveDamage: function(amount, from){
  return; //immortal
},
```

Listing 5.6. Impact corridor.

Corridor is type B that checks against type A (our player). Its receiveDamage() has been overloaded to do nothing (in case something accidentally does assign it damage). Its check() function looks to see if other is EntityPlayer. If so, the special Impact function loadLevelDeferred() is called. This waits until the end of the update cycle and properly deconstructs our level and loads the next one specified.

In this example, we are loading a level created by Weltmeister. Similar to the entity naming format, all levels created by Weltmeister are in the format Level<Name Of Level> with the first letter of the level name capitalized. We have created a tolevel variable so we can change the level being loaded from within Weltmeister.

5.6   Weltmeister

Before starting on the player entity, now is an appropriate time to draw the first level with Weltmeister. We have enough information to put together a collision map/tile map. The level needs to come before the player because development of an entity as complex as our player entity will not go far without putting it in a level.

If you unzipped and dropped in your Impact directory as-is on to your web server, then your Weltmeister installation can be reached at: http://localhost/your_dev_directory/weltmeister.html

Weltmeister will scan your game/lib/entities directory for *.js files. If you followed the naming structure stressed throughout the chapter, it will find your entities and make them available to you in the editor. See the screenshot in Figure 5.10 for a level in progress. If you are having problems with Weltmeister, make sure you have PHP working.

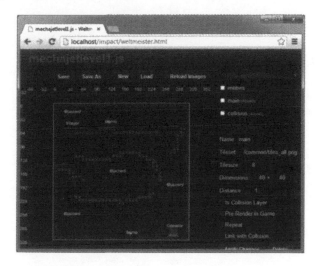

Figure 5.10. Weltmeister building level 1.

When first going to Weltmeister, you will be presented with a blank screen with the always-available "entities" layer. The first thing you will want to do is select this entities layer and then press the space bar to see if all the entities you created in game/lib/entities are available. If they are, press space to cancel and then use the plus symbol near the top right to create two more layers and rename them. You will eventually have these three layers named "entities," "main," and "collision." As you create these layers, you are given these options:

Name

The name of the layer. Note that the name "collision" is reserved for the collision layer.

Tileset

Select the image that represents your tiles.

Tilesize

It must be square. The default is 8, meaning 8 × 8 pixels.

Dimensions

Decides the size of your layer. The size is measured by tile size. A 20 × 30 dimension with a tilesize of 8 will be a 160 × 240 layer.

Distance

Determines scroll speed. "1" will scroll the same speed as the entities. "2" will scroll slower, and "3" will be even slower. This can be used to give a parallax scrolling effect.

Pre-Render in Game

Will pre-render your map. This can improve performance. The trade-off is that your tiles cannot be animated.

Repeat

Will repeat your tiles as it scrolls by. This can be used to create a repeating background effect.

Is Collision Layer

States the layer is a collision layer and will start using collision tiles allowing you to draw a collision map. Impact comes with a set of collision tiles you can use with your main layer tile set.

Link with Collision

Will allow you to create tiles that automatically have a solid collision tile behind it located on the collision layer. This can save you some mouse clicks.

Once your layers are configured, save your level. The convention is to save Impact levels into the directory lib/game/levels. Weltmeister will append ".js" to the name.

You are now ready to draw a level. First, you will probably want to draw collision tiles around the border to prevent the player from falling off the world. When working with the level editor, space will display the entity/tile selection box. Click to select. Then left click to paint. Holding right-click, drag the view around on your screen. Use the mouse wheel to zoom.

To erase an entity, click the entity layer (if not already selected), and then press the delete key. Erasing tiles is not so obvious. To erase a tile, click the appropriate layer, then press space to display tile selection, and then look at the top left corner of your tile selection box. There is a blank highlighted tile standing alone. Click the blank highlighted tile. Now paint the blank tile over the tiles you want to delete. This will delete them.

You now know the basics to build a level, but before we move on, here are a few handy keyboard shortcuts.

- The "z" key is undo.

- You can quickly clone an entity with the "c" key.

- You can copy a tile by clicking it while holding down the shift key.

- You can copy multiple tiles by dragging while holding down the shift key.

5.7   main.js

Like the name suggests, main.js is the entry point of the game. It contains the logic necessary to initialize the canvas, key binding, load the first level, and then start the game. Actually, right now, it won't load the first level because Weltmeister just created it, and main.js does not yet know it exists. See Listing 5.7 for the minimum amount of code to launch your level with keyboard and mouse binding.

```
ig.module(
  'game.main'
)
.requires(
  'impact.game',
  'game.levels.mechajetlevel1',
  'game.entities.player'
)
.defines(function(){
  MyGame = ig.Game.extend({
    init: function() {
      ig.input.bind( ig.KEY.UP_ARROW, 'up' );
      ig.input.bind( ig.KEY.DOWN_ARROW, 'down' );
      ig.input.bind( ig.KEY.LEFT_ARROW, 'left' );
      ig.input.bind( ig.KEY.RIGHT_ARROW, 'right' );
      ig.input.bind( ig.KEY.MOUSE1, "CanvasTouch" );
      ig.input.bind( ig.KEY.X, "xkey" );
      this.loadLevel(LeveMylevel);
    }
  }
});
// 60fps, 320x240, scaled by 2
ig.main( '#canvas', MyGame, 60,480/2 ,320/2 , 2 );
});
```

Listing 5.7. Impact main.js header.

Our level has been added to `requires`. It is the path to the JavaScript file. Then we launch our level inside `init`. Note the name that Weltmeister gave the level. You can always open the JavaScript file of the level to find the name.

Though these events do not do anything yet, we also binded the mouse, keyboard, and touch to our game. The reaction to these events will be processed in the player entity. For now, we need to add our arrow buttons so non keyboard users have control. We will be using the technique discussed earlier. These buttons are managed outside Impact entities. See Listing 5.8.

```
leftButton: {x:0,y:320/2-32,1:32},
rightButton: {x:32,y:320/2-32,1:32},
upButton: {x:16,y:320/2-64,1:32},
downButton: {x:480/2-32,y:320/2-32,1:32},
xButton: {x:480/2-32,y:320/2-64,1:32},

collisionDetect: function (object1, object2)
{
  //Same used in Tic-Tac-Toe
},
buttonCheck: function(theButton) {
  if(!ig.input.state("CanvasTouch"))
    {
    return false;
  }
  return this.collisionDetect(theButton, ig.input.mouse);
},
hudSheet: new ig.Image( 'fadedarrow.png'),
draw: function() {
  this.parent();
  this.hudSheet.drawTile( this.leftButton.x,
    this.leftButton.y, 4, 32 );
  this.hudSheet.drawTile(this.rightButton.x,
    this.rightButton.y, 1, 32 );
  this.hudSheet.drawTile( this.upButton.x,
    this.upButton.y, 0, 32 );
  this.hudSheet.drawTile( this.downButton.x,
    this.downButton.y, 3, 32 );
  this.hudSheet.drawTile( this.xButton.x,
    this.xButton.y, 2, 32 );
```

Listing 5.8. Impact main.js header.

First, you will create the buttons as objects. This makes them easier to track and pass in to our collisionDetect() function. The collisionDetect() function is our standard bounding box check identical to what was used in Tic-Tac-Toe. We have to use our own collision detect because the arrow buttons are not entities. buttonCheck() simply checks to see that the mouse/touch is actually occurring before calling collisionDetect. Finally, the draw function was overloaded to draw our arrow keys after it finishes drawing the other sprites.

5.8   Player Entity

Our player entity wraps up all the techniques we used for the Bomb (a death
sequence) and Buzzard (movement) as well as adding more (projectiles, control,
and respawn). First, we will add just enough code so the player can be placed
in the game by Weltmeister. See Listing 5.9.

```
ig.module(
    'game.entities.player'
)
.requires(
  'impact.entity'
)
.defines(function() {
EntityPlayer = ig.Entity.extend({
  size: {x:16, y:16},
  gravityFactor: 7,
  type: ig.Entity.TYPE.A,
  checkAgainst: ig.Entity.TYPE.B,
  flip: false,
  collides: ig.Entity.COLLIDES.PASSIVE,
  animSheet: new ig.AnimationSheet( 'robot.png', 16, 16 ),
  init: function( x, y, settings ) {
    this.parent( x, y, settings );
    this.addAnim( 'idle', 0.1, [0,0] );
    this.addAnim( 'roll', 0.1, [0,1] );
    this.addAnim( 'fly', 0.1, [12,13] );
    this.addAnim( 'death', 0.7, [24, 25,26], true );
  }
});
});
```

Listing 5.9. Impact player header.

Our entity doesn't do anything, but at least Weltmeister can see it, and
we can put it in our level. With our sprite available, we will be developing
main.js and player.js to make all the controls available. Because we've already
binded the keyboard and tracked buttons in main.js, we add the control logic
to the player.js. There is a lot of sprite manipulation happening with the
movement. Our player can roll, fly, or fall. This can happen in either direction.
Therefore, we need to keep track of the flip state and if the player is on the
ground and swap out animation accordingly. For clarity, only the X button
and left buttons are shown in Listing 5.10.

```
update: function() {
    //ig.log(this.friction.x, this.vel.x)
    if( ig.input.state('left') || this.leftButtonDown) {
        this.accel.x = -100;
        if(!this.vel.y)
        {
            this.friction.x = 35;
            this.currentAnim = this.anims.roll;
        } else {
            this.friction.x = 0;
            this.currentAnim = this.anims.idle;
        }
        this.currentAnim.flip.x = true;
        flip = true;
    }
    if(!this.vel.y && !this.vel.x)
    {
        this.currentAnim = this.anims.idle;
        this.currentAnim.flip.x = flip;
    }
    if( ig.input.state('xkey')  || this.xButtonDown ) {
        var bulletsettings = {flip:this.currentAnim.flip.x};
        //this forces 1 bullet at a time
        var alreadythere =
            ig.game.getEntitiesByType( EntityPlayerBullet )[0];
        if( !alreadythere ) {
            this.shootSound.play();
            ig.game.spawnEntity( EntityPlayerBullet,
                    this.pos.x, this.pos.y, bulletsettings);
        }
    }
    this.parent();
},
```

Listing 5.10. Impact player header.

Note that we are modifying the velocity variable like we did with the buzzard. Impact will look at the velocity and update the sprite on each frame accordingly, saving us a lot of hassle. Also, we are modifying friction. If we are in the air, we turn off friction. Otherwise, we slow down if we are on the ground. Additional variables have been added (leftButtonDown, xButtonDown, etc). These values are from the arrow sprites triggered by mouse/touch and are passed to the player from main.js.

The other piece to notice is spawning EntityPlayerBullet whenever X key or button is pressed. This entity is created in the same file just as we did buzzardboom and bombboom. The only difference is passing the flip state so we know which direction the bullet was fired. Lastly, we call this.parent() so impact can update the entity.

Now, we need to modify main.js to pass the touch and mouse clicks. See Listing 5.11.

```
.requires(
  'impact.game',
  'game.levels.mechajetlevel1',
  'game.levels.mechajetlevel2',
  'game.entities.player'
)
/* REMOVE FOR CLARITY */

update: function() {
  this.parent();
  // screen follows the player
  var player = this.getEntitiesByType( EntityPlayer )[0];
  if( player ) {
    this.screen.x = player.pos.x - ig.system.width/2;
    this.screen.y = player.pos.y - ig.system.height/2;

    //track button pushes
    player.leftButtonDown =
        this.buttonCheck(this.leftButton);
    player.rightButtonDown =
        this.buttonCheck(this.rightButton);
    player.upButtonDown =
        this.buttonCheck(this.upButton);
    player.downButtonDown =
        this.buttonCheck(this.downButton);
    player.xButtonDown =
        this.buttonCheck(this.xButton);
  }
}
```

Listing 5.11. Impact player header 2.

There are a few things happening in the new main.js update function. First, we added the player entity to our requirements list. Next, in the update function, we fetch the player entity. Impact fetch returns an array. We only need the first. We check to see if the player exists. If it does, we center the screen on the player. Because we are doing this constantly with every update, this will have a smooth-scrolling effect. Impact is well optimized to handle smooth scrolling for this simple game, but note that a more efficient strategy would be to scroll only when the player is near the edge of the screen.

Finally, we check the state of our buttons with the collision checks we added earlier. The player looked at these button states in its update function back in Listing 5.10. The bullet-spawning section we added will need to be commented out, but other than that, our player should now be able to move around the screen by keyboard, mouse, or touch. The gravityFactor will cause the player to fall, and the collision tiles will cause the player to stop when it lands on a platform.

We are now ready to add the player's bullets. See Listing 5.12 for the bullet entity.

```
EntityPlayerBullet = ig.Entity.extend({
  size: {x:16, y:16},
  collides: ig.Entity.COLLIDES.PASSIVE,
  type: ig.Entity.TYPE.A,
  gravityFactor: 0,
  checkAgainst: ig.Entity.TYPE.B,

  animSheet: new ig.AnimationSheet( 'bullet.png', 8, 8 ),

  check: function( other ) {
    other.receiveDamage( 10, this );
    this.kill();
  },

  update: function() {
    this.parent();
    if( this.vel.x == 0) {
      this.kill();
    }
  },

  init: function( x, y, settings ) {
    this.parent( x, y, settings );
    if(settings.flip)  {
      this.vel.x = -100;

    } else {
      this.vel.x = 100;
    }
    this.addAnim( 'idle', 0.1, [0,1] );
  }
});
```

Listing 5.12. Impact player header 3.

EntityPlayerBullet is essentially a reduced version of EntityBuzzard. The only needed changes were changing type B to type A, checkAgainst to type B, and the sprite sheets. As mentioned earlier, settings.flip looks to see which direction to travel. The check function has been overloaded to give 10 damage to whatever it hits and then call its own kill function.

Next, we need to add the player death sequence. Unlike with BuzzardBoom or BombBoom, we want the player to respawn. Rather than killing the player and then immediately spawning a one-off death entity, the player is going to show its own death sequence. See Listing 5.13.

The kill() function has been overloaded for the death sequence. Instead of dying, player.dead has been flagged true and the parent kill function has been saved to killcallback. Collision has been turned off. killTimer has been started.

```
kill: function(){
  ig.game.startXY = this.startXY;
  this.killTimer = new ig.Timer();
  this.killTimer.reset();
  this.killcallback = this.parent;
  this.dead = true;
  this.collides = ig.Entity.COLLIDES.NONE;
},
update: function() {
  if(this.dead)
  {
    this.vel.x = 0;
    this.vel.y = 0;
    this.currentAnim = this.anims.death;
    this.currentAnim.flip.x = flip;
    if( this.killTimer.delta() > 2 ) {
      this.killcallback();
      this.restartSound.play();
      ig.game.spawnEntity( EntityPlayer,
          ig.game.startXY.x, ig.game.startXY.y);
    }
  } else {
```

Listing 5.13. Impact player respawn.

During the update function, all the normal player interactions have been bypassed so the only thing that happens is the death animation gets played. After 2 seconds, this.killcallback() gets called to complete Impact's kill() process. The restart sound gets played and another player entity is immediately spawned to the original starting location.

5.9   Level 2

The first level of MechaJet is now playable. However, when the Corridor is reached, there is no level 2. The game will crash. We need to go back to Weltmeister and create a 2nd level. See the screenshot in Figure 5.11.

Level 2 is built the same way as level 1. The actual level is not important. Look in the bottom far right. Corridor is selected. Inside the corridor parameters there are "Key:" and "Value:" fields. These let you overload default parameters declared in the entity. Remember the tolevel property declared when first programming the Corridor entity (Listing 5.6)? We are now overloading the default value from within Weltmeister. This will cause this corridor to go back to level 1 when it is reached. Any field can be overridden this way. This feature allows a great level of flexibility within Weltmeister.

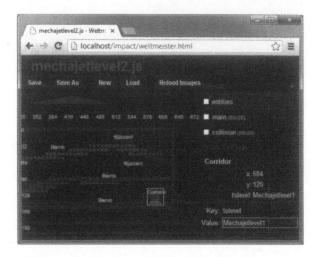

Figure 5.11. Weltmeister building level 2.

With level 2 built, it needs to be added "main.js" so it knows what to load when told. See below:

```
ig.module(
  'game.main'
)
.requires(
  'impact.game',
  'game.levels.mechajetlevel1',
  'game.levels.mechajetlevel2',
  'game.entities.player'
)
```

This completes the game. The player will go to the 2nd level when reaching the 1st corridor, and the player will be sent back to the 1st level when reaching the 2nd corridor. However, from a game design standpoint, the game is arguably not fully complete. There is no way to "win" the game. It is an endless loop from level 1 and level 2. However, it is complete enough for our tech demo.

5.10   Summary

In this section, we built MechaJet for Impact. We looked at the Impact folder structure and Impact's general way of doing things, particularly with getting our Entities to work with Weltmeister, the Impact level editor. From there, one-by-one, we created each entity and put them in our level. We then created our 2-level simple action side-scroller that can be controlled by keyboard, mouse, and touch.

A topic that didn't get touched on is Impact's built-in debugger. By including the debugger in the requires list, the Impact debugger will be launched and shown as you play your game. See below:

```
ig.module(
  'game.main'
)
.requires(
  'impact.game',
  'game.levels.mechajetlevel1',
  'game.levels.mechajetlevel2',
  'impact.debug.debug',
  'game.entities.player'
)
```

The information shown includes direction vectors, object counts, FPS, draws, etc. This information can be really helpful to fine-tune your game's performance. To remove this information, comment out the line in the requires list.

Next is our final, most complex (in both setup and development), game engine: The 3D Turbulenz game engine.

Chapter 6

Turbulenz

6.1   Source Code

All of the source code and examples are available at the website http://HTML5GameEnginesBook.com/. All the code, graphics, and sound are licensed free for personal and commercial use (MIT and CC-BY-3.0). Turbulenz is MIT licensed.

6.2   Introduction

Turbulenz is an MIT-licensed open-source (as of version 0.26+) HTML5 JavaScript/TypeScript game engine developed by Turbulenz Limited [91]. It is the only game engine featured that is powered by WebGL. Though some engines may allow WebGL to be used as an alternative choice for rendering, Turbulenz is WebGL at its core. This aspect has pros and cons which will be addressed in this chapter. Turbulenz is large, complex, and very powerful. The SDK (software development kit) encompasses many aspects of game development. Beyond the normal libraries developers would expect from a large HTML5 game engine, such as image, sound, animation, and physics, it also contains API to save games, generate stats, and even a payment system that connects to the Turbulenz services [94]. These extra services will not be covered.

6.3   WebGL

All our HTML5 game demos thus far were 2D and powered by HTML5 Canvas. However, not technically part of HTML5, but often included when discussing, many browsers offer 3D support in the form WebGL. WebGL is based on OpenGL ES 2.0 and is maintained by the Khronos Group, the same maintainers of OpenGL [72]. OpenGL ES is a mobile-optimized subset of the normal OpenGL standard that has been available on desktop computers for decades [73]. OpenGL ES 2.0 is the most popular revision because it is available on Android and iOS devices since 2009. However, up until recently, accessing the OpenGL features did not occur in the browser. The function calls were only available in that platform's native development environment (such Java, Obj-C, C++).

With WebGL, we can now have a hardware-accelerated 3D API available directly in the browser. As of this writing, WebGL availability is sparse and only within 2012+ versions of the Firefox and Chrome (not IE 10) desktop web browsers and limited support in Chrome/Firefox for Android. Still, 3D hardware acceleration is a welcome addition, and support should only improve. For now, if you as a developer wish to use WebGL, then you must accept that your audience will be limited to mostly non-IE desktop users. That is still a massive audience for your game, and mobile (and IE) will eventually catch up. Microsoft has already announced IE11 will support WebGL [95], so IE may be included in your test cases by the time you read this book.

This chapter bypasses direct WebGL to let Turbulenz handle the heavy lifting. If you want to dive deeper with a lower-level API, take a look at the popular "three.js" library located at http://threejs.org/.

6.4   Installation

Because this project is developing very quickly, be sure to look at http://docs. turbulenz.com/installing.html for the latest instructions. As of this writing, the best way to get Turbulenz is to download and install their SDK installer directly from the source located at GitHub (https://github.com/turbulenz/ turbulenz_engine). They perform regular releases of the SDK, but personal development has shown that it leaves out a couple useful features, such as the python scripts found in "manage.py". Installation from source is long and tedious. Both methods will be detailed here. Try the official installer first. Note that if you are only looking for game engine libraries (Protolib), the official SDK releases are more than sufficient.

6.4.1   Official Installer

Official installers are located at http://hub.turbulenz.com/. It requires free registration. Follow the registration procedure and download and install their SDK. The version in Windows uses a standard executable. The Mac version uses an install script. There are several noteworthy points about the Turbulenz SDK:

1. **It will install 32-bit Python 2.7 (if on Windows).** Note that this is not the latest version of Python. Python 2.x is a legacy support branch and is the version bundled with Mac (particularly version 2.6 for Mountain Lion, though 2.7 is made available [96]). The reason for 2.x is because Python 3.x breaks some backwards compatibility for various structural enhancements [92].

2. **Microsoft Visual Studio** is optional. The from-source version requires it. Note that Visual Studio Express is a free version (with Microsoft account registration) that can be downloaded from the web.

3. **For Mac, Xcode is required**. You do not need an iOS or Mac dev license. Turbulenz needs the command line tools from it. This can be found by going to Xcode → Downloads → components and then install "Command Line Tools". Xcode can be downloaded from the Mac App Store.

4. **Turbulenz installs a web server for you** (called the "Local Development Server"). It is running on port 8070. You can use XAMPP/-MAMP/WAMP instead, but the official development server is highly desirable to be able to test against Turbulenz back-end services. You do not need to move your www directory. The local development server is capable of serving any Turbulenz project local to your machine. The local development server is also preconfigured with lots of helpful samples.

5. **It will ask to install the Turbulenz plugin**. Turbulenz operates in Canvas mode and Plugin mode. The plugin is a browser extension used to enhance performance for browsers that happen to have the plugin installed. The game will fall back to Canvas mode if the plugin is not available.

After installing:

- For Windows, find "Run Local Server" in your Start menu. It should launch a console web server. See Figure 6.1.

- For Mac, execute "your_install_directory/start_local.sh" in your terminal.

• Go to http://127.0.0.1:8070/ in a recent web browser.

Figure 6.1. Turbulenz web server.

There are lots of samples running on the local server. Flip through and take a look at them. Note that some of the engine was written in TypeScript. TypeScript is an open-source superset of JavaScript developed by Microsoft [93]. One of the pitfalls of flexible interpreted languages, such as JavaScript, is that optimization is tedious. TypeScript introduces classes, interfaces, modules, and optional static typing. This allows easier development for large-scale projects as well as the ability to detect problems at compile time (thus, saving tedious hand-testing development time). Because TypeScript compiles to JavaScript, the language choice is seamless to the end user. TypeScript has often been compared to Dart and CoffeeScript because they also compile to normal JavaScript [97, 98].

This book does not dive into TypeScript. However, it is a nice language, and you may find yourself needing to look at it or wanting to use it for more serious Turbulenz (or other large web app) development. Regardless, at minimum, you will probably want syntax highlighting. Microsoft offers official TypeScript support for Visual Studio (Windows only) or Sublime Text 2 (for Windows and Mac).

6.4.2 Protolib

Protolib is the JavaScript object that encompasses a large portion of the Turbulenz SDK. You will be using protolib (and jslib) a lot to develop your game. If you do not wish to connect to Turbulenz's backend services and want only a nice game library, then these libraries are what you need. You can copy them off the sample apps and build a respectable game with just them (like the rest of Turbulenz, they are MIT licensed). However, we are going to continue on and use standard Turbulenz build procedures.

6.5   From Source

Installing from source is an involved process, but it guarantees you will have everything. Clone the GitHub project located at https://github.com/turbulenz/ turbulenz_engine. These are the commands you need to run:

```
git clone git://github.com/turbulenz/turbulenz_engine.git
cd turbulenz_engine
git submodule update --init
```

This clones the Git repo, navigates to the directory, and initializes the submodules. This will take a few minutes. Once it completes, close your Git shell if you are using Git Bash. It is no longer needed. The following commands will be with a normal command prompt. If you do not have the Visual Studio compiler, you should get it now. Also, the next steps require virtualenv. It is possible that you already have virtualenv because it is common to bundle it along with Python. However, it is not bundled with the official Python installer from python.org. First check to see that you have virtualenv installed. To do this, run

```
C:\Python27\python.exe -m virtualenv --version
```

That should output a version number. If you do not have virtualenv installed, run this next set of commands to install it:

1. Download http://python-distribute.org/distribute_setup.py

2. C:\Python27\python.exe your\download\path\to\distribute_setup.py

3. Download https://raw.github.com/pypa/pip/master/contrib/get-pip.py

4. C:\Python27\python.exe your\download\path\to\get-pip.py

5. C:\Python27\Scripts\pip.exe install virtualenv

This will install pip, a handy python installer tool. Then, it uses pip to install virtualenv. Test your virtualenv again with:

```
C:\Python27\python.exe -m virtualenv --version
```

With virtualenv ready, continue the installation with:

```
C:\Python27\python.exe manage.py env
env\Scripts\activate
```

This will fetch and set up and activate your local environment. After you are finished, you should see "env" next to your command prompt. See Figure 6.2.

Figure 6.2. Turbulenz env prompt.

You are now in the development environment. Python should be available locally. Next, we need to build all the tools and samples. Run these commands to build the remaining tools, apps, docs, and samples. This is the portion where the Visual Studio compiler will be called. The tools are smart and should detect which version you have installed (2008, 2010, or 2012 with update 2 installed).

```
python manage.py jslib
python manage.py tools
python manage.py docs
python manage.py samples
python manage.py apps
local_server --init
```

Setup has been completed. Launch the local development server with:

```
local_server --launch
```

You may want to use a second window to leave the local development server running. Note that whenever you launch a command prompt, you need to navigate to the Turbulenz source directory and run "env\Scripts\activate" to activate the development environment. This includes launching the web server.

Launch your web browser and go to http://127.0.0.1:8070/. You should see the Turbulenz dashboard and sample apps and games. You have now replicated the setup from the installer in the previous section. The rest of this chapter assumes you installed from source.

6.6   Hello Turbulenz App

With the installation steps out of the way, it is time for some code. Buried in your installation SDK under "apps" is a directory called "protolibtemplateapp" (If you wish to use an even deeper base, you could copy "protolibsampleapp" instead.) Make a copy of the directory in the same location of the other samples. Rename the directory to something reasonable, such as "helloworld". Next, build the app with this command (from the virtual environment; always use the virtual environment.):

```
python manage.py apps apps\helloworld
```

Turbulenz will invoke the build script. If you wish to add your app to the standard build list used during installation, open "manage.py", jump to around line 250, and add your game to this python list:

```
app_dirs = [ 'samples',
             'apps/inputapp',
             'apps/multiworm',
             'apps/sampleapp',
             'apps/templateapp',
             'apps/viewer',
             'apps/helloworld',
             'apps/protolibsampleapp']
```

Now, the "build all" command, "python manage.py apps" will build yours along with all the others. Next, we need to add this game to the local Turbulenz server. Assuming you left the local server running, navigate to http://127.0.0.1:8070/.

1. Click on plus button.

2. Paste the absolute path of helloworld in "Game Directory" (such as C:\Users\Dev\helloworld_engine\apps\helloworld).

3. Change the title and the slug to the name of your game, such as "Hello World".
   The slug will auto-update. The slug is the unique web path, such as "localhost/helloworld".

4. Save your game. You should see your new app.

5. Click your app. Click play. Click "canvas.debug.html".

Congrats! You have Turbulenz running a game. The game does nothing, so let's fix that. Open scripts/app.js and modify "initFn" and "updateFn" with these lines in Listing 6.1:

```
init: function initFn()
{
    var protolib = this.protolib;
    var mathDevice = protolib.getMathDevice();
    protolib.setClearColor(mathDevice.v3Build(0, 0, 0));
    // Intialization code goes here
    whiteV3 = mathDevice.v3Build(1, 1, 1);
},
update: function updateFn()
{
    var protolib = this.protolib;
    // Update code goes here
    if (protolib.beginFrame())
    {
        // Render code goes here
        protolib.drawText({
            text: "Hello World!",
            position: [protolib.width / 2,
                protolib.height / 2],
            scale: 10,
            alignment: protolib.textAlignment.CENTER,
            v3Color: whiteV3

        });
        protolib.endFrame();
    }
},
```

Listing 6.1. Turbulenz Hello World.

With this bit of code, we cleared the screen (using `setClearColor`) and added a draw routine (`drawText`) into the Tubulenz game loop. Refresh the page (if you are using the release version, you will need to recompile). You should see a white "Hello World!" centered on the screen in big font. The result is in Figure 6.3.

Figure 6.3. Hello Turbulenz.

We are now ready to begin development of a real app.

6.7 Turbulenz Game Structure

Like all the previous game engines reviewed, Turbulenz has its own way of doing things. These are the key directories and files to be kept at the front of your mind:

deps.yaml
> This contains the listing of assets used by your game. If you want to include any graphics, audio, etc, reference it in this file. The build script will give it a hash in **mapping_table.json** and copy it to the **static-max**/directory. The "staticmax" directory contains files told by the browser to very aggressively cache, which is why the file names are hashed.

> The deps.yaml file also is used by the build script when running "python manage.py apps apps\mygame". If the build sees a missing file, it will look in your turbulenz_engine\assets for a copy to bring forward.

manifest.yaml
> This contains all the game's meta information used by the Turbulenz server. Most of the time, you will be configuring this file via the Turbulenz web interface. This is where the changes are saved. It contains path, slug, cover art file, deployment information, etc.

templates
> This directory contains the HTML and script logic to build the header and footer, and says which JavaScript to include for your game. Once it is configured, it should not need to be touched except when another JavaScript library needs to be included or surrounding HTML structure is changed.

scripts/app.js
> This file contains your game logic. You will spend most of your time here.

app.canvas.debug.html and app.canvas.release.html
> "app.canvas.debug.html" points to the external "scripts/app.js" to allow simply refreshing the page file to test changes. "app.canvas.release.html" uses the packed and minify version for distribution. You need to recompile to test changes against app.canvas.release.html.

That is the bird's-eye view of the files most edited when working with Turbulenz. For more information, the docs are an invaluable resource. They are located at http://docs.turbulenz.com/.

6.8   Sky Marble Implementation

In this chapter, we will develop our final example game called "Sky Marble."
Here is the problem statement:

> "Sky Marble is a marble drop game that requires dropping boxes
> to center falling marbles on the screen without losing any."

See the screenshot in Figure 6.4. Sky Marble is quite complex. It contains
a 3D mesh, 3D rotations, 2D physics, sprites, build scripts, a game loop, and
more. This implementation has been reduced for clarity and will be described
by its major functions.

Figure 6.4. Sky Marble.

6.8.1   Init Function

Protolib represents a large slice of the SDK, and it is the go-to object for
declaring and configuring game-wide globals (not site-wide globals; Turbulenz
is very careful to not leak globals). Because there is no clear-cut place to store
game globals, I devised my own method of following Turbulenz's pattern of
attaching to the Protolib object. See the code below.

```
init: function ()
{
  var protolib = this.protolib;
  protolib.globals.gamevars = {};
  protolib.getGameVar = function(ref)
  {
    return this.globals.gamevars[ref];
  };
  protolib.setGameVar = function(ref, obj)
  {
    this.globals.gamevars[ref] = obj;
  };

  protolib.setGameVar("score", 0);
  protolib.setGameVar("gameover", false);
  //get example
  var score = protolib.getGameVar("score")
```

Turublenz already has "protolib.globals". Furthermore, I reserved myself "protolib.globals.gamevars". Many developers attach their semi-globals to "this", but I sometimes find "this" hard to track when deep inside a function. By attaching to protolib, I just need to keep track and fetch protolib, which is quite often needed anyway. The rest of the initialization is very Turbulenz boilerplate. See Listing 6.2.

```
var mathDevice = protolib.getMathDevice();
var graphicsDevice = protolib.getGraphicsDevice();
var floor = Floor.create(graphicsDevice, mathDevice);
var soundDevice = protolib.getSoundDevice();

var darkV3 = mathDevice.v3Build(51/255,51/255,51/255);
protolib.setClearColor(darkV3);

// Intialization code goes here
var phys2D = Physics2DDevice.create();
protolib.globals.draw2D.configure({
    viewportRectangle: [0, 0, viewPort.width, viewPort.height],
    scaleMode: 'scale'
});

var world = phys2D.createWorld({
    gravity: [0, 2]
});

protolib.setPreDraw(
    function ()
    {
        floor.render(graphicsDevice, protolib.globals.camera);
    }
);
```

Listing 6.2. Turbulenz initialization.

Here is what is happening block-by-block:

setClearColor accepts a Vector3 object with x, y, z representing R, G, B in the range of 0 through 1. Web developers are used to thinking in terms of 0 through 255 for our colors. This is simple enough to fix. Just take your normal decimal value and divide by 255.

mathDevice provides 3D vector and matrix operations. Without getting into too much detail, a matrix is a series of numbers arranged in rows and columns. They are used all over 3D graphics for positioning, movement, and rotation. In this example, we are using 2D Physics with just a splash of 3D for some nice effects.

graphicsDevice contains all the methods related to managing the rendering of the game to the screen. In the above code, it was set to the viewport width and height and told to scale with the browser. It is not used directly except in this example to render the floor to create a nice effect.

soundDevice is based on the Open Audio Library and supports a plethora of variables, effects, filters, etc. This is beyond the scope of the book. For our purposes, soundDevice provides an easy way of detecting whether "ogg" or "mp3" should be loaded. See below:

```
var soundExt = ".mp3";
if (soundDevice.isSupported("FILEFORMAT_OGG"))
{
    soundExt = ".ogg";
}
protolib.setGameVar("winsound",
  "sounds/win_effect" + soundExt);

//play the sound
protolib.playSound({
   sound : protolib.getGameVar("winsound")});
```

The choices are `FILEFORMAT_MP3`, `FILEFORMAT_OGG`, or `FILEFORMAT_WAV`.

Physics2DDevice This creates our "World", the root object that holds all our other objects. This is identical to the notion of a "stage" used in EaselJS.

For Turbulenz, instead of adding objects to our stage, we are now adding them to our 2D "World". We also pass a 2D gravity parameter that states a vector of X = 0 and Y = 2. Our objects will fall downward. The gravity vector could point anywhere to make some interesting games.

protolib.setPreDraw() is the place to put objects to be drawn below everything else (the bottom layer when thinking of 2D). We are putting the floor here. The floor serves no real purpose except as a nice visual effect (and as an excuse to demonstrate this function). Displaying the floor is normally used for debug/development.

Our game features a 3D rotating torus (a 3D donut-shaped object) for a nice effect. Below is the code that creates it:

```
var torusMesh = {};
torusMesh.meshPosition = mathDevice.v3Build(0, 2, 0);
torusMesh.meshPositionForward = mathDevice.v3Build(0, 0, -0.05);
torusMesh.meshPositionBackward = mathDevice.v3Build(0, 0, 0.05);
torusMesh.meshPositionDirection = torusMesh.meshPositionForward;
torusMesh.meshRotationMatrix = mathDevice.m43BuildIdentity();
torusMesh.meshRotateX = Math.PI * 2 - Math.PI / 2;
torusMesh.xAxis = mathDevice.v3BuildXAxis();
torusMesh.mesh = protolib.loadMesh({
    mesh: "models/torus_.dae",
    v3Position: torusMesh.meshPosition,
    v3Size: mathDevice.v3Build(10, 10, 10)
});
protolib.setGameVar("torusMesh", torusMesh);
```

Turbulenz is the only featured game engine in this book that can handle 3D objects exported with 3D graphics animation software, such as Autodesk Maya or Blender. It accepts a translated COLLADA formatted scene/object, usually represented as a ".dae" file. COLLADA is an open 3D format maintained by the Khronos Group, the same maintainers as OpenGL and WebGL [99]. It was designed to be a transition format between other 3D systems. Turbulenz does not load COLLADA files directly. It converts it to a JSON (**Ja**va**S**cript **O**bject **N**otation) format as part of the build process and then puts it in "staticmax". Loading and processing 3D objects is a fairly expensive browser operation, so keep that in mind when using 3D objects.

The above code simply sets up a 3D Torus, a primitive ring shape in 3D designs. It then sets up a rotation matrix around the X axis. This will cause the mesh (a collection of vertices and edges that represents a 3D object) to rotate as time passes creating a nice effect. Try changing "v3Build**X**Axis" to "v3Build**Y**Axis" to see a different rotation. The meshPositionDirection variable tracks the movement direction inside the game loop.

Next, the game floor is set up as 0.1 tall (just enough to add a little texture) and 2 * viewport-wide box at the bottom of the screen:

```
var solidFloor = {};
solidFloor.width = viewPort.width * 2;
solidFloor.height = 0.1;
solidFloor.position = [0, viewPort.height ];
solidFloor.phys2DPolygon = phys2D.createPolygonShape({
    vertices: phys2D.createBoxVertices(solidFloor.width,
        solidFloor.height)
});
solidFloor.phys2DBody = phys2D.createRigidBody({
    type: 'static',
    shapes: [solidFloor.phys2DPolygon],
    position: solidFloor.position
});
world.addRigidBody(solidFloor.phys2DBody);
```

Turbulenz supports three rigid bodies, and they are each featured in the game. They are "static", "kinematic", and "dynamic" [100]. Static bodies cannot move, which is why it was chosen for our floor. Kinematic bodies are like static, except they can be moved around the screen. They are appropriate for player-controlled entities. Dynamic bodies react to the world's physics. They are used for the marbles and bricks.

Developers familiar with the Box2D physics engine should recognize the terms "static","kinematic", and "dynamic". Box2D uses the exact same terms for its bodies [101] and they have the same meaning. Turbulenz's 2D physics engine is not Box2D, but it follows many Box2D patterns.

Next, to set up the 3D camera:

```
protolib.setNearFarPlanes(0.1, 100);
protolib.setCameraPosition(mathDevice.v3Build(0, 2, -4));
protolib.setCameraDirection(mathDevice.v3Build(0, 0, 1));
protolib.setAmbientLightColor(mathDevice.v3Build(1, 1, 1));
```

This sets up the player's view of the 3D scene. The camera is offset a little bit and looking directly in the center at our torus. This allows the floor to show. Play with these variables to see how very useful the floor can be in development. The ambient color is white. Changing this value will affect the glow color of the torus.

The last initialization step is our event listener. We are only using desktop mouse clicks. Turbulenz supports a "touchstart" event, and it is set up in a similar fashion, but as of this writing, mobile support is extremely limited. Only the desktop mouse version is presented below. By the time you get this book, you may be ready to investigate mobile support.

```
inputDevice.addEventListener('mousedown',
    function (mouseCode, x, y)
    {
        protolib.setGameVar("eventPositionX", x);
        protolib.setGameVar("eventPositionY", y);
        if (mouseCode === mouseCodes.BUTTON_0)
        {
            protolib.setGameVar("mouseClicked", true);
        }
        if (mouseCode === mouseCodes.BUTTON_1)
        {
            //right mouse for testing
        }
    }
);
```

Like in our other games, the mouse location is saved and put in a variable so it can be used later during the game loop. With this, the game has been initialized. Other than spinning and moving the torus around, the rest of the game is 2D physics with marbles and bricks. These functions are presented in the next sections.

6.8.2   dropBrick/dropMarble/updateTorus Functions

See below for `dropMarble(x,y)`. `marbleArray` is the array that holds all the marbles.

```
marbleArray[i] = Object();
marbleArray[i].width = 3;
marbleArray[i].height = 1.75;
marbleArray[i].marblecolor = "textures/redmarble.png";
marbleArray[i].position = [ x , y ];
marbleArray[i].phys2DPolygon = phys2D.createCircleShape({
    radius : 1,
    origin : [ 0, 0]
});
marbleArray[i].phys2DBody = phys2D.createRigidBody({
    type: 'kinemetic',
    shapes: [marbleArray[i].phys2DPolygon],
    velocity : [0.8 * ((marbleArray.length % 2) ? -1 : 1), 0],
    position: marbleArray[i].position,
    angularVelocity : Math.floor(Math.random()*11)
      * ((marbleArray.length % 2) ? -1 : 1)
});
world.addRigidBody(marbleArray[i].phys2DBody);
```

This is initialized similar to the floor, except an array is used because the game is tracking multiple marbles. Also, we are creating rigid kinemetic circles (`createCircleShape` instead of `createPolygonShape`) to add to our world. Width, height, and position are self-explanatory. The velocity alternates left and right. The marble comes out spinning with a strong random angular velocity and also alternates direction. We also save the red marble texture (used later).

Like most 3D engines, Turbulenz is particular about texture dimensions. The image has to be square and a power of two (32×32, 64×64, 128×128, etc) [102].

`dropBrick(x,y)` is nearly identical. `brickArray` holds all the bricks. The relevant part is presented below:

```
brickArray[i].phys2DPolygon = phys2D.createPolygonShape({
    vertices: phys2D.createBoxVertices(1, 1)
});
brickArray[i].phys2DBody = phys2D.createRigidBody({
    type: 'dynamic',
    shapes: [brickArray[i].phys2DPolygon],
    mass: 50,
    position: brickArray[i].position,
    angularVelocity : Math.floor(Math.random()*11)
      * ((brickArray.length % 2) ? -1 : 1)
});
world.addRigidBody(brickArray[i].phys2DBody);
```

A 1×1 kinemetic box is being created in the same way as the floor. It has the same spin as the marble. The biggest difference is the mass is huge at 50. This makes the drop effects very splashy.

Next, we need to rotate and move the torus using `updateTorus()`:

```
torusMesh.meshRotateX += (Math.PI * 4 / 360);
torusMesh.meshRotateX = (torusMesh.meshRotateX % (Math.PI * 2))


mathDevice.m43SetAxisRotation(torusMesh.meshRotationMatrix,
   torusMesh.xAxis, torusMesh.meshRotateX);
torusMesh.mesh.setRotationMatrix(torusMesh.meshRotationMatrix);
torusMesh.meshPosition = mathDevice.v3Add(torusMesh.meshPosition,
   torusMesh.meshPositionDirection);
torusMesh.mesh.setPosition(torusMesh.meshPosition );
```

This is just adding 2 degrees to the rotation. If the accumulation exceeds 360 degrees (PI * 2), the modulus operator resets it by taking the remainder. Note that JavaScript's modulus operator works for floating point. The other line adds "torusMesh.meshPositionDirection" to the position. Later in the code (not shown), boundaries are checked to make the torus fly the other direction when it passes the camera. The important piece of logic is below:

```
if (Math.round(torusMesh.meshPosition[2] * 100) == -400 ) {
for(var i=0; i< marbleArray.length; i++) {
    if (marbleArray[i].marblecolor
        == "textures/bluemarble.png") {
        continue;
    }
  var pos0 = Math.round(marbleArray[i].position[0] * 10);
  var pos1 = Math.round(marbleArray[i].position[1] * 10);
  if (pos0 > 95 && pos0 < 105 && pos1 > 45 && pos1 < 55 ) {
      marbleArray[i].marblecolor = "textures/bluemarble.png";
      protolib.setGameVar("score", score + 1);
      this.dropMarble(Math.random() * (16 - 2) + 2,1);
      protolib.playSound({
        sound : protolib.getGameVar("winsound")});
  }
}
```

For the very brief moment as the torus flies over, if there is a red marble in the center of the screen, it will turn the texture blue and add a point to the score. It then plays a sound and drops another marble. This is the core piece of game logic. From trial and error, these hard-coded values made for the best user experience. Hard numbers are sufficient for a tech demo, but further abstraction would use percentages based on screen width, height, and marble size.

This method of moving the torus by directly manipulating position values is essentially teleporting it around and is not recommended. For a smoother animation, a 3D physics simulator could be used and the torus could be given a Z velocity. This also would allow the engine to handle collision detection for us if needed. However, our physics is 2D, and the torus is not colliding with anything anyway. Thus, we move it manually because the code is easier (for us and the browser).

That concludes the helper functions. Next is the actual game loop.

6.8.3   Update Function

Our game loop takes place between physics frames. Inside it, we look for events, such as input and gameover. We also draw our scene. Turbulenz, like our other examples, uses immediate mode rendering [103], so we need to draw our scene every frame. This update function has been reduced for clarity.

```
update: function ()
{
  if (protolib.beginFrame())
  {
    if (mouseClicked && !gameover) {
        var x = eventPositionX / protolib.width * viewPort.width;
        var y = (eventPositionY / protolib.height)
                * viewPort.height;

        protolib.playSound({
            sound : protolib.getGameVar("hit1")});
        protolib.setGameVar("mouseClicked", false);
        this.dropBrick(x, y);
    }

    gameTime += protolib.time.app.delta;
    protolib.setGameVar("gameTime", gameTime);
    while (world.simulatedTime < gameTime && !gameover)
    {
        world.step(1/60);
        this.updateTorus();
    }
}
```

The first section looks to see if a mouse button is pressed (the mouseClicked flag was set during the actual event). The math is scaling the mouse click location to the in-game coordinates. The viewport width is 20 while the mouse click can range from 0 to whatever the browser size may be. Thus, it needs to be scaled.

The next bit of code is tricky. After adding all the objects to the physics world, we need to tell the simulator to perform its calculations. This is done with the step() function. The function is locked in a while loop with the total simulation time compared to the total real time (by accumulating time deltas). If the physics is behind, the while loop will cause it to catch up with the current time (at a simulated rate of 60 FPS). Looping to catch up is a very common task with physics simulations.

This technique allows the game flexibility to run at 60 FPS on strong hardware and smoothly scaled down to a slower speed (such as 30 FPS) if that is all that can be handled.

Next, we need to draw the bricks, marbles, and floor. The bricks and marbles code look nearly identical, so only the marble is presented because it has a twist.

```
for(var i=0; i< marbleArray.length && !gameover; i++)
{
    marbleArray[i].phys2DBody.getPosition(marbleArray[i].position);
    protolib.draw2DSprite({
        texture: marbleArray[i].marblecolor,
        position: [marbleArray[i].position[0]
            - marbleArray[i].height / 2 -0.1,
          marbleArray[i].position[1]
            - marbleArray[i].height / 2-0.1],
        width: marbleArray[i].height+0.2,
        height: marbleArray[i].height+0.2,
        rotation: marbleArray[i].phys2DBody.getRotation()
    });

    if (marbleArray[i].position[0] < -2
      || marbleArray[i].position[0] > (viewPort.width + 2))
    {
        protolib.setGameVar("gameover", true);
    }
}
```

We are drawing a 2D texture on top of a 2D body. Note that the function being named Sprite is a bit misleading. As stated before, this function draws a texture that must have dimensions in the powers of 2. The -0.1 and +0.2 sprinkled around the widths and positions are fudges to make the square peg (brick) fit inside the round hole (marble).

The other point to consider is the gameover event. Our circle has a radius of 1. If it rolls to a position of -2 or a viewPort.width+2, then it has gone off the screen. That is gameover.

The solid floor (not shown) is identically placed. The difference is that there is only one floor, so there is no loop.

With that, our game is complete.

6.9   Other Turbulenz Tips

6.9.1   Debugging

Chrome's debugger allows executing functions directly from the console. This is very handy. However, if you properly scoped your variables to not leak globals, then you may be at a loss on how to access this functionality.

Turbulenz has its own method of debugging. Take a look at this code:

```
protolib.addWatchVariable({
    title: "Score",
    object: protolib.globals.gamevars,
    property: "score",
    options: {
        min: 0, max: 100,step: 1
    }
});
```

Assuming you are using the default template, this will put a slider in the debug area to let you dynamically modify the `score` variable of the object `protolib.globals.gamevars`. Slide the bar left and right to see the score change. Any variable can be exposed to a slider like this. This is a very useful debugging tool.

6.9.2 Templates

To customize the surrounding HTML, the layout is located in "templates". The app is currently loading the default built-in template. To extract this default template and make it your own, run this command (from the virtual environment):

```
(env) C:\Users\dev\turbulenz_engine>makehtml -D \
    -o default_modified.html
```

Put that file in the same directory, and tell templates\app.js to import your own template:

```
/*{% extends "default_modified.html" %}*/
```

The app should load identical as before, but you can now fully customize the surrounding HTML by modifying default_modified.html.

6.10 Summary

In this section, we built a 2D game using a 3D engine and 2D physics. Though our game was structurally 2D, we leveraged the 3D engine to sprinkle some visual enhancements that would not have been possible with the other engines. This allowed us to touch a bit on 3D game development topics, such as textures, meshes, and matrix transformations.

We learned about WebGL and its pros (impressive graphics) and cons (very limited support). Fortunately, the main detriment, limited support, will eventually go away.

Turbulenz has a very high learning curve, and it will probably take until late 2014 before a large mobile audience has the hardware available for it. However, the performance of Turbulenz is top notch, and the price (free and open source) can't be beat. Eventually, all the browsers will catch up with it, and your games can be ready for them to use it.

This concludes the tour through the different game engines. In Part III, you will learn how to package an HTML5 game for distribution. The promise of HTML5 as an app can be written once and run anywhere. Right now, that is true if they are online and using a web browser. What if the player wants to play offline? What if we want the player to find our app in Google Play or iTunes? How about allowing it to be played outside of a browser?

These distribution scenarios will be covered in Part III.

Part III

HTML5 App
Distribution

Chapter 7

Chrome Web Store

7.1 Source Code

All the distribution project files and examples are available at the website http://HTML5GameEnginesBook.com/. All the code, graphics, and sound are licensed free for personal and commercial use (MIT and CC-BY-3.0).

7.2 Introduction

If you have followed the guides in any of the previous chapters, then you have successfully written a game that can run on nearly all computers and mid-to-high-range mobile devices being manufactured in 2012 (except, perhaps, Turbulenz).

But there is slight caveat to that statement: The player has to be online and direct their browser to the site serving the game libraries every time they want play. This inconvenience is the main motivation for an entire third part to this book. After all, the game is just JavaScript and media files. Once the web server hands over the files, its job is done. The player could disconnect immediately.

The purpose of Part III is to look at various ways to get the game into the hands of players. We want the player to be able to find and install the game without having to visit our obscure website every time they want to play it. We want the player to be able to find our game through all the major app centers they already know and trust. We want the player to be able to play the game even if they aren't online.

In this chapter, we will look at distributing our game as a desktop app through the Chrome Web Store. In this example, we will be using MechaJet from Part II (page 75), but any game supported by Chrome will do (which is all of our example games).

7.3 Chrome Web Store

Chrome Web Store can best be described as "Google Play but for apps on the web." It has also been described by critics as "a solution looking for a problem [64]." Looking at just purely a technical spec list, the critics may be correct. After all, why ask the user to install an app when the actual site is just a bookmark away?

Yes, perhaps internet power users have little need for an app store for their web apps, but let's ignore the critics for a brief moment and look at the bigger picture. The Chrome Web Store has significant gains beyond giving us the simple "offline mode". That's gravy. What it really gives us is yet another avenue for users to find (and possibly buy) our game. With an API (application programming interface) that's so easy to use, a potential audience of hundreds of millions of users (the store is available on every new desktop Chrome browser tab), and a registration fee of just $5 [65], there is simply no reason to leave our game out of it.

7.4 From Web App to Chrome App

7.4.1 Getting Started

Chrome Web Store apps begin life as a normal web app. This may seem obvious, but if you are coming from the land of Android or iOS development, you often create the app first and then the website second. With the Chrome Web Store, create the web app first. We've done that already with MechaJet. With our fully functioning web app, we will now make it into a Chrome app. The first step is:

- Give the app a permanent home.

This can be a subdomain of a normal domain (like myapp.blogger.com) or the root domain. Google will ask you to verify ownership of the site. There are various ways to verify ownership. The easiest method is to upload an .html file they give you. Having a website for the app is not a technical requirement. This is for Google to tie your app to a site.

The next step is:

- Create icons and images.

Submitting to the Chrome Web Store requires several images:

1. App icon that is 128 × 128 named "icon_128.png".

2. At least 1 screenshot that is 1280 × 800 or 640 × 400.

3. At least one promotional banner that is 440 × 280.

See the Tools Appendix on page 175 for image software that may help you in creating these icons. These images all have associated guidelines beyond just pixels. Also, the app submission page requires text and other requirements. Expect to spend a day creating images and gathering information to submit your app. For now, we are only concerned with bundling up our app into a developer package. For that, we only need the app icon.

Next step is:

- Create a Manifest.

Those who have worked with Android development will be familiar with the term "manifest". It is a file that makes declarations about the overall app package. Google Play requires it for Android apps, and Chrome Web Store requires it for Chrome apps. The Chrome Store version is much easier. It is simply a JSON file. There are several items that are required.

1. Name of app

2. Description of app

3. Version of app

4. manifest_version, which is currently "2"

5. Icon we mentioned earlier

6. A launch specification (either local_path or web_url)

The manifest.json used in our example is printed in Listing 7.1. It is the bare minimum required to package the app and let it run locally.

```
{
  "name": "HTML5 Game Engines Book  Demo",
  "description": "MechaJet demo game",
  "version": "0.0.0.1",
  "manifest_version": 2,
  "icons": {
    "128": "icon_128.png"
  },
  "app": {
    "launch": {
      "local_path": "index.html"
    }
  }
}
```

Listing 7.1. Chrome manifest.json.

Our app would be classified as a "Packaged App." Chrome also supports "Hosted Apps" for online games. This may actually be more fitting for your needs if your game needs a lot of server-side management. The user will visit our site and Chrome can store the necessary information to be able to play portions of the game offline. To get you started, Listing 7.2 is an example of such a manifest.

```
{
  "name": "HTML5 Game Engines Book Demo",
  "description": "MechaJet demo game",
  "version": "0.0.0.1",
  "manifest_version": 2,
  "icons": {
    "128": "icon_128.png"
  },
  "app": {
      "urls": [
          "*://chrome.html5gameenginesbook.com/"
      ],
      "launch": {
          "web_url": "*://chrome.html5gameenginesbook.com/"
      }
  },
  "offline_enabled": true,
  "permissions": [ ]
}
```

Listing 7.2. Chrome web app manifest.json.

The difference between "Packaged App" versus "Hosted App" is mostly one of permissions. If your app requires extension-level changes to the browser experience and always-on functionality (such as notifications), you will need a packaged app.

Our Chrome app is now finished. The next step is to install it.

7.4.2 App Development

"App Development" is different from the Chrome Developer Tools mentioned on page 39. To enable the app developer mode in Chrome, click the "Customize" icon in the top right and then navigate to Tools → Extensions. Then enable Developer Mode.

From there, you can load your unpacked extension. This will immediately tell you if your manifest JSON is well-formed and valid. If you are having problems http://jsonlint.com/ is a nice free JSON validation tool.

Go to your apps tab and you should see your 128 × 128 app icon. Click it, and if all is well, you will be taken to your game in full offline glory! From this extension page is also where you pack your extension into a ".crx" for distribution. You also can click to reload an unpacked extension to help your development.

7.5 Summary

With just 14 lines of additional code, a few extra images, and the help of Chrome, we turned our HTML5 game into a desktop app that can be played offline. Submitting it to the Chrome Web Store will give us access to millions of Chrome users. As of May 2013, there are 750 million desktop and mobile Chrome users [82].

In the next chapter we will look at the more involved task of using Ejecta to package MechaJet into an app that can go into the Apple App Store for distribution to iOS devices.

Chapter 8

Apple iOS App Store

8.1   Source Code

All the distribution project files and examples are available at the website
http://HTML5GameEnginesBook.com/. All the code, graphics, and sound are
licensed free for personal and commercial use (MIT and CC-BY-3.0). Ejecta
is MIT licensed. The Impact engine is proprietary and is not distributed.

8.2   Introduction

If you wish to have your app run standalone on an iPhone or iPad, there is
simply no other choice than to put it in the Apple's iOS App Store. Whereas
Android, Windows (non-Windows 8 UI style [77]), and Mac allow multiple
distribution channels, Apple only allows its store for iOS devices. Fortunately,
packaging an HTML5-based app for the Apple App Store is a mostly solved
problem. Every game engine goes out of its way to make sure it is well
supported, sometimes even improving over normal browser performance during
the packaging process. This chapter investigates using the Ejecta framework
to improve performance. Note that Google Play Store distribution, discussed
in the next chapter (page 143) features CocoonJS, which can target iOS as
well. If you are targeting both platforms and wish to have a one-size-fits-all
approach, you may wish to skip to the next chapter.

   Before diving into complex process of device provisioning and setting up
Ejecta, note that Apple provides a shortcut method to hosted web apps wanting
to provide a more native experience. See the HTML meta tags below:

```
<meta name= "viewport"
  content= "width=device-width,initial-scale=1.0">
<meta name="apple-mobile-web-app-capable" content="yes">
```

These meta tags were introduced back in section 2.5.1 on page 38. These tags allow the user to create a shortcut that will launch a full-screen Mobile Safari for a more native-like experience. The upside is that this takes just two minutes to implement. The downside is losing the potential performance improvements provided by Ejecta, and the app cannot be run offline. A complex HTML5 game will need the acceleration provided by Ejecta (discussed later), but this trick could be used for less intense web apps or as a baby step until the full app is available.

8.3   Device Provisioning

If you wish to test your app on an iOS device, you must purchase an iOS developer license from Apple [78]. It is currently $99 per year. The simulator is currently free, and the Xcode tools are currently free from the Mac App Store. That can get you pretty far, and performance is pretty decent for a simulator. However, there is no substitute for real hardware running the app, particularly with game development. This section will describe how to get an app onto your device for testing. If you wish to stick with the simulator and save some cash, then skip over to section 8.4. Note that you will eventually have to purchase an iOS developer account if you wish to publish to the Apple App Store.

To get your app onto hardware, you must provision your device. To do this, you need your Unique Device Identifier (UDID) for the device. Follow these steps:

1. Connect your iPhone/iTouch/iPad to your computer.

2. Launch iTunes. Let it connect to your device.

3. Select your device in the left sidebar. If you don't see a sidebar, you can enable it in the "View" menu.

4. Find your serial number in the main window. See Figure 8.1. Click your serial number. Your UDID will be revealed. See Figure 8.2.

5. Right click or Command+C to copy it to your clipboard and save it for later.

Figure 8.1. iPad iTunes SN.

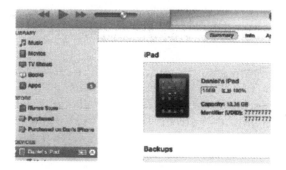

Figure 8.2. iPad iTunes UDID.

Armed with your UDID, you are now ready to provision the device for development. You are allowed to provision up to 100 devices with one developer account. Launch a browser and navigate to https://developer.apple.com/ and go to iOS Dev Center. Near the top right, click the link to go to "Certificates, Identifiers & Profiles". From there click "Provisioning Profiles". If you have not registered and purchased a $99 per year iOS Developer account, you will be required to do so during the course of navigating. Once in the portal, you are now ready to begin the fairly complex task of setting up an iOS device and app for testing and distribution.

iOS provisioning comes in two profiles: Development and Distribution. Distribution is covered later. For now, you want to create a "development" profile. Follow Apple's walk-through as your certificates and profiles get generated, saved, uploaded, downloaded, and attached to your Mac's Keychain along the way. Apple and your Mac will jointly generate the various files you need. Here is what will happen. Naturally, if the process has changed, follow Apple's steps over this one:

1. Launch Keychain Access and request a certificate.
   This can be done by going to Spotlight Search → "keychain" to launch
   Keychain Access. Then go to Keychain Access → Certificate Assistant →
   Request a Certificate. Fill out the form and save the certSigningRequest
   file to your disk.

2. Submit the certSigningRequest file to Apple in the portal.
   The place you submit it will be in iOS Developer Portal under "Certificates". This is the same area where you found the instructions to create
   it.

3. Download and install the generated certificate.
   Once you upload it, you will be taken to a place that says "Pending".
   Because you are the owner of the account, it is implicitly approved. Wait
   20 seconds and refresh the page, and then you will see a download link.
   Download the cer file and then double-click it to install it to your Mac's
   Keychain.

You are now set up with a paid iOS development profile and certificate.
You now need to create an App ID and add your iPhone or iPad to your
development profile. Go to App IDs, click the big plus sign, and fill in the
information. The only recommendations are that using a wildcard makes
development easier. However, wildcard bundle IDs are not supported with in-
app purchasing. Also, by convention, bundle IDs use reverse-domain notation
(com.example.myapp.ios). This bundle ID will be used in your app within
Xcode. Now, go to "Devices" and add your iOS device by submitting a common
name and the UDID that you copied earlier. Click Save.
   Now, on to the final step: the actual development profile. Here are the
steps:

1. Select that you are making a development profile.

2. Select that App ID you made earlier.

3. Select the certificate you made earlier.

4. Select the iOS device you added earlier.

5. Name the profile.

6. Download the generated mobileprovision file. Double-click to install.

That was quite complicated, but all the pieces are now in place. Download
Xcode from the Mac App Store if you do not already have it. Connect your
iOS device if it is not already connected. Launch Xcode and then navigate to
Window → Organizer. The Organizer utility will launch. Click "Devices" at

the top and then "Provisioning Profiles" on the left. Click "Refresh" on the bottom right, and then Xcode will fetch your information from Apple. See the screenshot in Figure 8.3. In the screenshot, there is also a distribution profile which you may not yet have. That happens when you are ready to publish, and the steps are exactly the same as development. The only difference is the certificate is submitted to the distribution section in the portal.

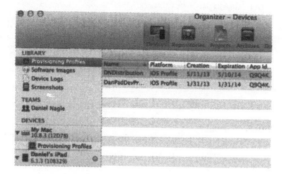

Figure 8.3. iOS provisioning profiles.

Now, enable development on your iOS device and attach your profile to it. See the screen shot in Figure 8.4.

Figure 8.4. iPad development enabled.

Finally finished. The iOS device should be recognized by Xcode and allowed to run the app within the device instead of a simulator. If it is not listed, try exiting out and then relaunching. Xcode does a fetch from Apple when it starts. If that doesn't work, check "Build Settings" under "Code Signing". We are now ready to build an HTML5-based game that can run native on iOS. To help us, we will be using the Ejecta framework.

8.4 Ejecta

Ejecta is an open source project by the same developer who maintains Impact [67]. Dominic describes it as: "A web browser that is Canvas-only." As expected, Impact is very well supported, but it also can be used for other engines with some caveats that won't be covered here (hint: avoid DOM. Use

Canvas). In this section, our Impact-based game, MechaJet, is a natural choice to use as an example.

8.4.1 Setup

Ejecta can be found at impactjs.com/ejecta. As of this writing, the official stable branch is at version 1.2, but as with many open source projects, the adventurous may download and work with the latest development branch. Currently, I have found that the latest master branch from GitHub seems to work best, so that is what will be described here despite the structure being slightly different.

First, we will set up the "Hello World" example that comes bundled with Ejecta. There are a lot of files and libraries associated with Ejecta. It is essentially a low-level optimized version of the JavaScriptCore engine used by Safari being bundled with your app. The root directory of a fresh Ejecta project looks like this.

App

> The directory that has your Canvas-based JavaScript app. You may need to create this directory. Inside this directory should be an "index.js" file that is the main entry point of your application. One was probably given when downloaded.

ejecta.xcodeproj
> The XCode project file.

Resources
> App icons and other settings not directly related to rendering the game.

Source
> Implementation of the Ejecta framework and lots of supporting libraries.

"index.js" needs more discussion. When your Impact game is "baked", index.js becomes your "game.min.js" and all is fine. However, you would be very lucky to get everything you need right with the first attempt. You will probably want to develop the game and optimize directly for Ejecta. For that, when your game isn't baked, your index.js points to your game libraries. See Figure 8.5.

Figure 8.5. Ejecta project file structure.

Notice the removal of Weltmeister. It is not needed. Also, the "Tools" is gone too. It's only used for baking. The contents of index.js is different as well. Instead of game.min.js, it is now just the two lines listed in Listing 8.1.

```
// Load the game
ejecta.include('lib/impact/impact.js');
ejecta.include('lib/game/main.js');
```

Listing 8.1. Ejecta index.js unbaked.

Note that just because Weltmeister has been removed doesn't mean it can't be used. The MAMP server supports remapping the web root "www" directory to another location. You could change your web root to a location so Weltmeister can access your Xcode project directories. Then you could modify your levels more easily. You can detect Ejecta within Impact by looking at "window.ejecta". Through these if-statements, you could eventually work towards a single universal build structure.

By now, the game should compile and run. The issues that may be found are probably screen size as Ejecta does a lot of scaling for you.

8.5 More Notes

A few important notes about working with Ejecta:

No Orientation Changes

Ejecta does not support changing orientation. In fact, as of this writing, it currently crashes the engine. Decide which orientation you want to support and set it under "Default Orientation" in your app settings.

No DOM

Ejecta's support for DOM specific calls, like `document.getElementById`, is extremely limited. Heavy DOM-oriented libraries, such as jQuery, cannot be used.

console.log

Your nice Chrome and Impact debugger tools are no longer available, but you still have trusty `console.log()`. It shows up in your normal Xcode output window.

8.5.1 Ejecta Audio

Ejecta supports MP3, M4A, and Apple's version of uncompressed audio (commonly known as "PCM" or "wav files") in a format called CAF [75, 76]. Apple recommends this audio strategy when developing an iOS application's sound effects [74]:

1. 30 seconds or less

2. In linear PCM or IMA4 (IMA/ADPCM) format

3. Packaged in a .caf, .aif, or .wav file

While Apple supports wav, we are restricted by Ejecta to the .caf format. For longer and looping sounds (e.g., background music), Apple recommends instantiating the AVAudioPlayer class. Ejecta handles this for us and will pick the appropriate method. MP3s are fine for background music, but this means we still need to solve our short audio problem. Apple has a command-line tool called "afconvert" that runs in Terminal that will get our short audio files into the format we need.

Here is an example conversion for our sound files:

```
afconvert -f caff -d LEI16@44100 -c 1 fireburn.mp3
afconvert -f caff -d LEI16@44100 -c 1 bombboom.mp3
afconvert -f caff -d LEI16@44100 -c 1 restart.wav
```

afconvert accepts a variety of formats. The above will generate the files "fireburn.caf", "bombboom.caf", and "restart.caf". Convert your sound effect audio files to CAF, and then modify the lines that launch your game to look as follows:

```
if( ig.ua.mobile && !window.ejecta) {
    // Disable sound for all mobile devices except Ejecta
    ig.Sound.enabled = false;
}

    var width = 1024/2;
    var  height= 768/2;
    var  ctx = canvas.getContext('2d');
```

```
ctx.imageSmoothingEnabled = false;
canvas.style.width = window.innerWidth;
canvas.style.height = window.innerHeight;
ig.Sound.channels = 2;
ig.Sound.use = [ig.Sound.FORMAT.CAF, ig.Sound.FORMAT.OGG,
    ig.Sound.FORMAT.MP3];
ig.main('#canvas', MyGame, 60, width, height, 1);

});
```

Before, we had sound disabled on mobile devices, now, we only disable it on mobile devices if Ejecta is not running. Impact lets you detect Ejecta by looking for "window.ejecta". Also, we are telling the Impact engine to use two sound channels and prefer the CAF format if available.

A couple other tweaks you will see is the scaling. We are now scaling at a factor of 1 and we changed the canvas dimensions to 1024/2 and 768/2, which is half the standard iPad dimensions. Then, we compensate by stretching the canvas to the same size of the screen. We switched to stretching the canvas instead of using the Impact engine for scaling because the author of Ejecta advised us to do that [75]. My personal experimentations showed little performance difference with Impact scaling versus Ejecta canvas, and the Ejecta scaling was a little more awkward to manage. However, we will defer to the recommendation of the maintainer of the tool. Note that the ability to change the canvas style attribute was just checked into GitHub less than one month before it was detailed in this book. The Ejecta project is moving very fast. Check it often, and test the latest.

With our dimensions and scaling changed, we need to fix button locations. They currently show up in the wrong places. See the fix below:

```
this.leftButton = {x:0,y:canvas.height-32,l:32};
this.rightButton = {x:32,y:canvas.height-32,l:32};
this.upButton = {x:16,y:canvas.height-64,l:32};
this.downButton = {x:canvas.width-32,
        y:canvas.height-32,l:32};
this.xButton = {x:canvas.width-32,y:canvas.height-64,l:32};
```

With that, our app is finished and can run natively on iPads.

8.6   Preparing for the App Store

There is a large amount of prep work to get an app into the Apple App Store. Initially, splash screens and icons need to be drawn in each resolution for all the supported iOS devices (iPhone, iPad, and the retina display variants). Assuming that is handled, we can go back to provisioning. This time it is for distribution.

8.6.1   Distribution

Navigate back to the Apple Provisioning Portal and follow the previous steps to set up a distribution profile. The steps are exactly the same as when you set up your development profile. State that the certificate is for distribution, not development. When finished, download and install the generated cer file. Next, follow these steps. They should look very familiar:

1. Create an App ID unique to that distribution.

2. Select the App ID you made earlier.

3. Select the certificate you made earlier.

4. Select the iOS device you added earlier.

5. Name the profile.

6. Download the generated mobileprovision file. Double-click to install.

Now, Xcode needs to be told to use the distribution provision. Launch Xcode and follow these steps:

1. Duplicate the "Release" configuration and rename it "Distribution". See Figure 8.6.

2. Select the "Build Settings" tab, and change the Code Signing for "Distribution" to use the distribution profile. See Figure 8.7.

3. Click the name of the project in the top left. This is the build scheme section. Create a new scheme called "Distribution". See Figure 8.8.

4. Xcode will switch to the Distribution scheme. Click the scheme, and then click "Edit Scheme...".

5. Select "Run Ejecta.app" (or whatever your app name may be) and choose the Distribution build configuration. See Figure 8.9.

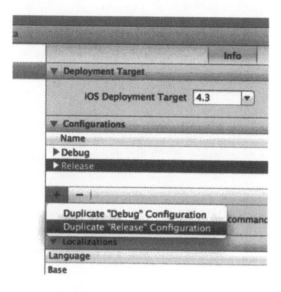

Figure 8.6. Xcode duplicate release.

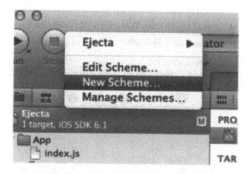

Figure 8.7. Xcode code signing distribution.

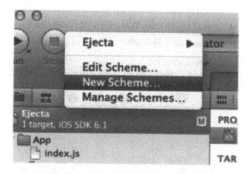

Figure 8.8. Xcode new scheme.

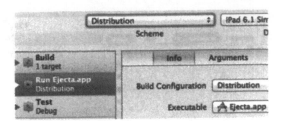

Figure 8.9. Xcode distribution build configuration.

Xcode is now properly configured with two schemes: One for development, another for distribution. When built, Xcode will generate a ".app" file for iOS. Its icon will look like Figure 8.10. This app cannot be run by Mac OS X. It is built for iOS.

Game.app

Figure 8.10. Xcode iOS distribution build.

8.6.2   iTunes Connect

When your final app is ready to be uploaded to iTunes, your next stop is over at iTunes Connect, located at http://itunesconnect.apple.com/. Login using your Apple credentials and navigate to "Manage Your Apps". Click "Add New App" and follow the steps. The only thing remarkable about this process is you may have another round of graphics to generate. When finished, your app will say "Waiting for Upload".

Back to Xcode. Select the distribution scheme. Select iOS device as the target. Then select Product → Archive. Xcode will build your app and Organizer will appear with your app icon. Next, click "Validate". Xcode will now validate and sign your app with the credentials stored on your Mac and created within iTunes Connect. If all goes well, you will get a success notification that looks like Figure 8.11.

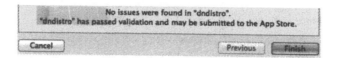

Figure 8.11. Xcode validation passed.

Next, click the "Distribute" button. This will invoke more code signing and eventually upload and place the app into iTunes for review. The status will eventually transition to "Waiting for Review". If your app is waiting for review and you change your mind, you can reject the binary. The navigation is iTunes Connect → "Manage Your Applications" → "View details" → "Binary Details". The "Reject this binary" button is in the upper right.

Apple does not specify a review schedule. Personal experience shows about two weeks before your app gets reviewed and published, and getting a rejection on the first attempt is pretty normal. Provide more information for the reviewer and fix the problems that were raised. The next attempt usually gets reviewed a lot quicker. Two days is normal. Updates to previously reviewed apps are also quicker, usually within five days.

8.7 Summary

Despite Android having the marketshare, iTunes has the mindshare. Often the question, "Is there an app?" is actually asking: "Is there an iPhone/iPad app?" Sometimes, a business has not really *arrived* until it has a published iOS app. Yes, it can be difficult to get into the Apple App Store, but working through the process is necessary to get your game in front of the very large and potentially lucrative iOS app market. Apple users are big fans of apps, and they are willing to spend money on apps that are quality. The great thing about HTML5 is that this crowd does not have to go unserved. There were very few technical aspects in this chapter. It was almost completely about the iTunes publishing process. Hopefully, after reading this chapter, it will feel a little less draconian and more like just a necessary evil.

The next chapter teaches how to package and submit an HTML5-based app to the Google Play Store for Android users.

Chapter 9

Google Play Store

9.1 Source Code

All the distribution project files and examples are available at the website http://HTML5GameEnginesBook.com/. All the code, graphics, and sound are licensed free for personal and commercial use (MIT and CC-BY-3.0). The Impact engine is proprietary and is not distributed.

9.2 Introduction

Despite accounting for roughly 70% of all smartphones worldwide [68], Android distribution always seems to be a second class citizen when it comes to game engine support. Game engine maintainers go far and out of their way to make sure iOS is well supported and Android becomes an afterthought. However, the game engine maintainers cannot be faulted entirely. Android development is very hard in that the number devices running on it are extremely varied, and each could be running a different version of the Android operating system, a problem called "fragmentation."

When an iOS developer finishes a game for the iPhone and iPad running the latest version of iOS plus one version back (a good development strategy), the developer can be assured that a very large majority of all iPads and iPhones can install and run their app. Android does not have that luxury. The only sure way to test is to build up a collection of tablets and phones with different Android versions and run the app. As HTML5 web developers, we are familiar with this test strategy by juggling browsers and operating systems inside virtual machines. Unfortunately, with Android, we are now juggling actual hardware. The Android development tools do have an Android emulator capable of launching a variety of Android test scenarios, but it is very slow and cumbersome. (Tip: For a better emulator experience, try an Intel-based Android image instead of ARM.)

Though the test strategy for Android may be complex, at least the build strategy is not that difficult. As mentioned before, game engine support is not quite as polished on iOS, but at least the tools that are available do work well. This chapter will get your HTML5-based game to run native on an Android device so it can eventually be distributed in Google Play or any other store.

Our targets are usually chosen for us when we use commercial HTML5-wrapping tools. If you are looking to build a standard Android app using the standard SDK tools, my personal recommendation is dial back no farther than Android 4.0. Android went through a lot of rapid changes from 2.x, 3.x, and 4.x. Google introduced a lot of standard themes and a native action bar system in 4.0. This is now the method of navigation users expect. Therefore, consider saving yourself a lot of backwards-compatibility hassle and start at 4.0. The glut of 2.3 Gingerbread users will eventually catch up.

9.3   CocoonJS

Last chapter, we used Ejecta for our Impact game, but Ejecta is not supported for Android. CocoonJS is a commercial HTML5 wrapper for both Android and iOS maintained by Ludei [69]. The setup is the same for each platform, so we could have just used CocoonJS for both Android and iOS, but that wouldn't have been as fun, would it? Also, CocoonJS uses its own "cloud" compiler. That means you upload your code to Ludei, and their server compiles your code. It then lets you download your final package. The pros and cons of being dependent on "the cloud" could fill an entire book. Here is a summary:

Cost
> CocoonJS is currently free, but it may not always be. CocoonJS also requires their logo shown during startup.

Internet
> CocoonJS requires an Internet connection to use. You may not always have stable fast connection during development.

Control
> CocoonJS uses its own compiler with its own capabilities. You may wish to have more, but you can only have what they give you.

Ejecta is free, open source, not dependent on an Internet connection, and doesn't require a splash screen. It is more difficult to set up, but these benefits make it worth it for the iOS version. However, there is the cost of having 2 build structures to maintain if you wish to support both Android and iOS. If you are willing to do the cost/benefit trade and be CocoonJS-only, you can make that decision.

9.3.1 Setup

As mentioned before, CocoonJS uses the cloud to compile code. Eclipse and the Android developer tools do not even need to be installed (though the Java Development Kit will be needed eventually to sign your apk (Android packaged kit) to upload to Google Play). However, you will want to keep MAMP, XAMPP, or WAMP to easily fetch the zip package and install it on your Android device. To get started, download and install the free CocoonJS launcher from Google Play. This is what you will use to locally develop and test your app. Once installed, you will need to register an account with Ludei. From there, Ludei will email you a registration code to enable the CocoonJS launcher.

After everything is configured and registered, your launch screen will look like Figure 9.1 (Nexus 7 being shown).

Figure 9.1. CocoonJS launcher.

CocoonJS comes with demo apps to install and test its system. These demo apps are also available from its website. They are invaluable in determining the CocoonJS methods and API for developing HTML5 games. Our game will need to be modified to work with their tools, which we will get to shortly. For now, download one of its sample games, put it on your local web server (MAMP, WAMP, etc.), and then download it using their launcher. See Figure 9.2.

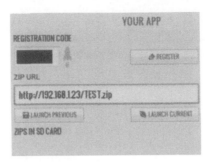

Figure 9.2. CocoonJS fetch app.

If everything is set up correctly, its demo app will download and launch. We can now begin the process of replacing its app with ours.

9.3.2   MechaJet on CocoonJS

Download the MechaJet project from the book's website. The only piece missing is the Impact engine (which cannot be distributed in raw form). Drop your Impact library into the normal "lib/" location. The example project is already set up to look for it there. Zip up the project, and then send it to the CocoonJS launcher. You should see MechaJet playing on your Android device. If you do not own a copy of Impact, there is a baked version of MechaJet available that also will launch and play using CocoonJS.

Backtracking starting with MechaJet from Part II, it is not a simple copy-paste-replace to get an Impact app running with CocoonJS. There are a couple tweaks to get the app to work. Particularly,

HTML
> CocoonJS has very minimal HTML support. Essentially, CocoonJS just gives us a blank web document. We have to create the Canvas manually. This is not so much different than the Ejecta framework from the last chapter.

Touch events
> CocoonJS has a little trouble with our HUD arrows. This is not a big deal. We just need to rewrite our touch handlers so CocoonJS understands them. That part of our game was removed from our Impact entities and made custom anyway.

If you were to load the desktop Part II MechaJet right now, you would get a blank screen. The first problem we need to solve is the missing canvas. To do this, we add these lines right before initializing the game. (See below.) While we are at it, we will enable audio again. Before, we had it disabled on mobile devices. CocoonJS supports it.

```
/* CocoonJS lets us have our audio back.
if( ig.ua.mobile ) {
    // Disable sound for all mobile devices
    ig.Sound.enabled = false;
}
*/
//create canvas for CocoonJS.
var c = document.createElement('canvas');
c.id = 'canvas';
document.body.appendChild(c);
//start game
ig.main( '#canvas', MyGame, 60,480/2 ,320/2 , 2 );
```

Now the game loads and runs. However, touch controls do not work. As
mentioned before, CocoonJS has trouble accepting our touch controls. We
need to add our own touch listeners. See the additions in Listings 9.1.

```
ig.touchLocation = Object();
ig.touchactive = false;
c.addEventListener(
  "touchstart",
  function(touchEvent) {
    var e= touchEvent.targetTouches[0];
    var touch = Object();
    touch['x'] = e.pageX/2; touch['y'] = e.pageY/2;
    ig.touchLocation = touch;
    ig.touchactive = true;
});

  c.addEventListener(
  "touchend",
  function(touchEvent) {
    ig.touchactive = false;
});

  c.addEventListener(
  "touchmove",
  function(touchEvent) {
    var e= touchEvent.targetTouches[0];
    var touch = Object();
    touch['x'] = e.pageX/2; touch['y'] = e.pageY/2;
    ig.touchLocation = touch;
    ig.touchactive = true;
});
```

Listing 9.1. CocoonJS touch impact.

We have added a listener to touchstart, touchmove, and touchend. We keep
track of this activity by adding new objects to the ig global object. We know
if it is active and we know the location. We can now change our buttons to
look at these to see if it needs to react. See this change below:

```
buttonCheck: function(theButton) {
/* OLD METHOD
    if(!ig.input.state("CanvasTouch"))
    {
        return false;
    } '
    return this.collisionDetect(theButton, ig.input.mouse);
*/
  // NEW METHOD
    if(!ig.touchactive)
    {
      return false;
    }
    return this.collisionDetect(theButton, ig.touchLocation);
},
```

Since we are tracking the touches ourselves, we remove Impact's CanvasTouch check and replace it with our own. Send the new parameter for the collision detect routine, and we are good to go. If we send the game right now to CocoonJS launcher, it will be playable. CocoonJS is heavily optimized for HTML5-based games, so our game runs at a good speed as well.

9.3.3 Generating an APK (Android Package Kit)

To create an apk suitable for native Android installation, you must use the CocoonJS cloud compiler. Login to their web service, create a project, fill out the form, and then upload the exact same zip package that you used for their launcher app. After a few minutes, you will receive an email with links to download your natively compiled apk. As mentioned before, you also can have it generate an iOS project from your zip package.

9.3.4 Distribution

Android apps are distributed as "apk" files. The apk file is simply a collection of files zipped. If you want to look inside it, you can easily append ".zip" and then open it with your file manager. Inside, you will find several Android-related directories and files, such as "assets", "META-INF", "res", "AndroidManifest.xml". Desktop Java developers may recognize this format since Java distributables, ".jar" files, are also zip files set up in a similar way.

Take a look inside "assets", and you will find the JavaScript files and other assets that contain your game. This brings us to the point of the exercise of opening up the Android package. There is little worry about extracting your game from an iOS device. Apple has gone to great lengths to remove a user's ability to do that. However, with Android, extracting an apk and unzipping it to get access to the JavaScript for your game is not a difficult task. Consider running your files through obfuscation or minify before final deployment (such as Impact's "baking", or UglifyJS used by Turbulenz). Naturally, the paranoid may have considered doing that anyway before uploading it to the CocoonJS Cloud compiler (their terms of service state they discard your source package after they compile).

Assuming you went through all the necessary JavaScript obfuscation techniques, we can proceed to putting this app in the Google Play Store. This process is easier than the Apple App Store.

9.3.5 Signing the APK

All Android apps must be signed before they are allowed on an Android device [87]. To aid debugging, Android devices allow debug-signed applications if "Unknown Sources" is checked on the device. Google Play will not allow a debug-signed apk into the store. Therefore, CocoonJS makes available two versions of the apk: One is debug-signed that can be used for testing. The other is unsigned ready to be signed and sent to Google Play (or other app store) [88].

Here is the signing process:

1. Install the Java Development Kit (JDK) if you do not have it. This will install Keytool and Jarsigner tools for you. If you have gone through the process of installing the Android SDK, then you already have the JDK.

2. Create a keystore to sign your apk. In Windows, the utility may be located in a place such as "C:\Program Files\Java\jdk1.7.0_21\jre \bin\keytool.exe". On Mac, it is located in "/usr/bin/keytool" and is probably available in our system path. The command is :

```
keytool -genkey -v -keystore mykey.keystore \
  -alias mykeyalias -keyalg RSA -keysize 2048 \
  -validity 10000
```

Replace the `mykey` and `mykeyalias` to something more appropriate. Do not forget the passwords or lose this keystore. This certificate and alias must be reused to sign all updates.

3. Sign your apk using jarsigner. The utility is located in the same place you found keytool. Here is the command:

```
jarsigner -verbose -keystore mykey.keystore \
  -storepass KEYSTOREPASSWORD -keypass KEYPASSWORD \
  unsigned_app.apk mykeyalias
```

Your app is now signed and ready for Google Play. Next:

1. Go to https://play.google.com/apps/publish/.

2. Fill out the forms and upload the required graphics.

3. Upload the apk binary.

If you have not done so, you will be prompted to pay the one-time $25 Google Play developer fee to list your app. Unlike Apple, there is no review process once your app is submitted. There is also no annual renewal fee. The pros and cons of a cheap no-review style app market versus Apple's process-heavy with higher fee-style app market is a very fruitful debate that will not be discussed here.

9.4 Summary

The Android market is massive. At Google's annual developer conference in March 2013, they announced 900 million Android activations to date and 48 billion app installs from Google Play [81]. As mentioned before, despite the huge install base and large app market, the mindshare and game engine support is still with Apple iOS. However, these numbers cannot be denied. Android is taking over the mobile world. Ignore the naysayers. Pay the extremely small $25 fee and make the effort to list your game in the store. Google has made the barrier to entry too small to dismiss. The problem of finding HTML5 compilers with good game performance will be solved. We have a good solution with CocoonJS now and more will come along.

The next chapter takes a break from devices and goes back to online distribution through Facebook.

Chapter 10

Facebook App

10.1 Source Code

All the distribution project files and examples are available at the website http://HTML5GameEnginesBook.com/. All the code, graphics, and sound are licensed free for personal and commercial use (MIT and CC-BY-3.0). However, for this chapter, it is recommended to use the Heroku base as your starting point for your game.

10.2 Introduction

The focus of Part III of this book is the various ways to run HTML5 apps offline and purchase them through app stores. Therefore, it seems odd to include a chapter about Facebook. Our games will not run offline with Facebook. However, the extremely large audience on Facebook (arguably the world's biggest web site [70]) trumps the offline requirement to be included in Part III.

We want our game in front of as many people as reasonably possible. Facebook attracts lots of gamers, and it would behoove us to have our game available to users within their preferred medium of entertainment, particularly if there is a strong social aspect to the game. Facebook is not difficult to support. Like the Chrome Web Store chapter, this chapter will be very process-driven.

10.3   Setup

Naturally, the first step is to get a Facebook account. Chances are high that you already have one (BTW, this book's Facebook page is located at http://facebook.com/HTML5GameEngines). The next step is to go through the developer registration process. Follow these steps:

1. Visit the Facebook Developer Page:
   Go to https://developers.facebook.com/apps. When you navigate to the Facebook developer portal, you will see either your dashboard if you have an app, buttons to create an app, or a "Register Now" button to get started. If you have not visited this page before, you will probably see Figure 10.1.

Figure 10.1. Facebook app landing.

2. Sign up as a Facebook Developer:
   Facebook developer system requires deeper verification than acknowledging an email. Fill out the related information and give Facebook your phone number or a credit card for identity verification. See Figure 10.2.

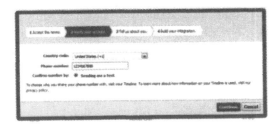

Figure 10.2. Facebook confirm phone.

3. Install the Developer App:
   The Facebook developer app is the starting point to getting apps on Facebook.

Once you work through the registration process, next time you visit the developer portal, your "Register Now" button will become a "Create an App" button. The welcome screen is now a dashboard. See Figure 10.3.

Figure 10.3. Facebook create new app.

Facebook has essentially developed its own language for developing web apps on its platform. They have a very rich and diverse API that can fill many books (and it does). One word used a lot is "Canvas." That is their term for content presented to users when they visit a page. We will be using a Facebook canvas to develop our Facebook game, and the Facebook canvas has little to do with our HTML5 canvas. Fortunately, we don't necessarily have to be too concerned with the bulk of the Facebook language (Graph API, Social Channels, Facebook Credits, etc.) to get our game loaded and running.

10.4   App Registration

Now that we are registered as a Facebook developer, we need to register our app. Click new app. Type in the name, namespace, and check if you would like free hosting by Heroku. Namespace is a unique identifier similar to Android and iOS app identification. The difference is that only letters and underscores are allowed. Finding a name that is not taken, particularly one called "test app", is difficult. You may need to get creative or just use gibberish if you are simply testing. See Figure 10.4. In this book, we will be using Heroku.

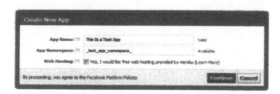

Figure 10.4. Facebook test app dialog.

10.4.1   Heroku Setup

Heroku has been the main app hosting partner for Facebook since late 2011 [71]. They have a diverse set of platforms to choose from, such as PHP, Python, Node.js, and Ruby. Node.js is a rare and welcomed choice from hosting providers. If you are building a multi-player game, which is common for social games, Node.js handles it well due to the architecture of the environment. This book does not go into detail about Node.js. Instead, we will be using normal PHP as our platform because we are already familiar with it after working with Impact. See Figure 10.5.

Figure 10.5. Facebook Heroku account.

Once you save and submit, your app will be created instantly, and you will be taken to its hosting page. It will look something like Figure 10.6, and your Facebook app setup page will look like Figure 10.7. Your Heroku page comes prepopulated with lots of useful Facebook features, such as logging in, seeing a list of users, and more. For our purposes, we are only keeping app login.

Figure 10.6. Facebook Heroku welcome.

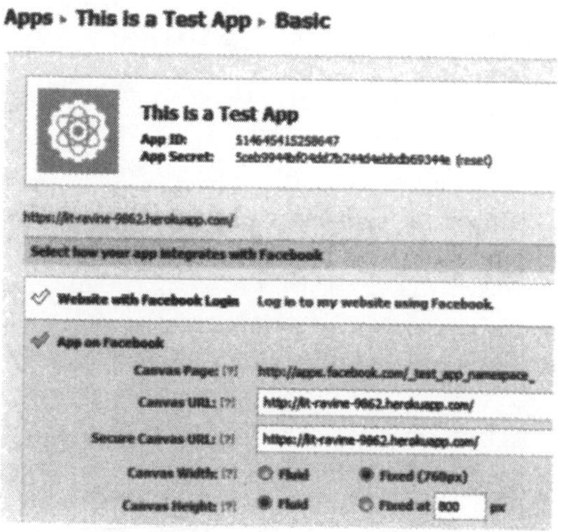

Figure 10.7. Facebook app setup with Heroku.

Heroku uses a toolkit (which they call "toolbelt") that includes SSH, Git (msysgit for Windows), and other utilities. They install into your system PATH and are used for developing and deploying your Facebook application. After installing their toolbelt, launch a command prompt and login. See Figure 10.8.

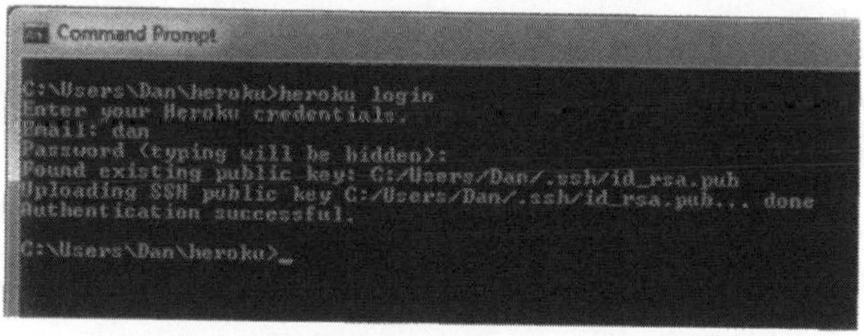

Figure 10.8. Heroku login.

Then immediately follow the login with the Git clone command sent to you in your registration email. Your Heroku system is ready for development. You can edit the sample source code and push it back to Heroku when finished ("git push heroku").

10.5   Tic-Tac-Toe on Facebook

Any game could run on Facebook. Our Tic-Tac-Toe game just happens to fit
well because Facebook IFRAME apps must run at 720 pixels width to not
need to scroll. Our Tic-Tac-Toe game runs at 600, so we are good. To get
our app in there, we need to load index.php and replace the content with our
game. Note that there is nothing particularly remarkable about this file. We
could just replace this with our entire tictacoe.html as-is, and it would work
fine. However, then we wouldn't be making use of Facebook's services.

First, find the JavaScript includes and add the CreateJS suite. See below:

```
<script type="text/javascript"
    src="/javascript/jquery-1.7.1.min.js"></script>
<!-- Added Tic Tac Toe-->
<script src="createjs-2013.05.14.min.js"></script>
<script  src="tictactoe_easeljs.js"></script>
```

Next, clear out the unneeded tags, the body "onload" event, and the login
link. See Listings 10.1. After you make the changes, run these commands to
push your changes to the server:

```
git commit -a -m 'your comment'
git push heroku
```

```
<body  onload="onload();">
    <h1>Welcome to Tic Tac Toe.
    <?php
      if ($user_id) {
    ?>

Draw an X.</h1><br>
    <canvas id="canvas" width="600" height="600"
     style="background-color:#000000"></canvas>


    <?php
      } else {
      ?></h1>
    <div class="fb-login-button"
      data-scope="user_likes,user_photos"></div>
    <?php
      }
```

Listing 10.1. Facebook Tic-Tac-Toe body.

If the user is not logged in, he will be presented with a login link that
launches the standard Facebook login window, as seen in Figure 10.9. If
the user is logged in, the canvas with Tic-Tac-Toe will be loaded, as seen in
Figure 10.10.

Figure 10.9. Facebook Tic-Tac-Toe not logged in.

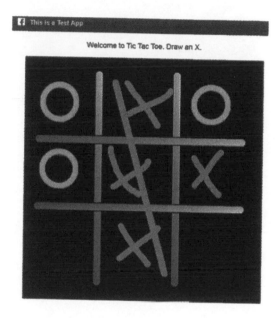

Figure 10.10. Facebook Tic-Tac-Toe logged in.

10.6 Summary

This short chapter did not touch any social aspects, which is one of the pillars of Facebook. Heroku includes the entire Facebook PHP SDK, JavaScript SDK, jQuery, and sample code widgets to get you going. Now that you know how to get a basic app running on Facebook, experiment with the API to add social aspects. Facebook puts your app in sandbox mode to help you develop so you can release when ready. Also, within the code, Heroku shows how you can run your app on localhost so you don't have to constantly push to their server. Experiment. Have fun with it.

The sample Tic-Tac-Toe game is included on the book's website, but you are encouraged to use Heroku's starting base instead. The next chapter is back to offline distribution through native desktop installers. It will cover both Mac and Windows.

Chapter 11

Windows and Mac Native

11.1   Source Code

All the distribution project files and examples are available at the website http://HTML5GameEnginesBook.com/. All the code, graphics, and sound are licensed free for personal and commercial use (MIT and CC-BY-3.0). Node-webkit is MIT licensed.

11.2   Introduction

The Chrome Web Store was a convenient way to quickly get our game into the hands of the millions of desktop Chrome users. However, despite the millions of users, there are still millions of desktop users not using Chrome and who are being left out. Also, even among the Chrome users, not everybody has a Google account and regularly visits the Chrome Web Store to be able to install our game.

Regardless of the reasons, it is possible to distribute an HTML5 app directly to the end user and bypass all the third parties. It takes a bit of extra effort, but the benefit will be ultimate end-to-end control of the user experience. The only requirement to play the game will be proper hardware with a supported operating system. This chapter will describe how to do this for both Windows and Mac using node-webkit, which does much of the heavy lifting. The bulk of this chapter will be building installers.

11.3 node-webkit

node-webkit is an MIT-licensed (which is free to distribute commercially) project on GitHub that is managed by Roger Wang and sponsored by the Intel Open Source Technology Center. It is based on a combination of Node.js and Chromium [83]. Having Node.js functionality in apps is interesting in its own right, but for our purposes, this project allows us a very convenient way to distribute our HTML5 web-based apps as normal desktop apps. Note that node-webkit predates the announcement where Chrome would fork Webkit to use the Blink rendering engine. Because node-webkit is based on Chromium, which technically does not use Webkit, the name of the project could possibly change.

To get started, download the Windows and Mac precompiled binaries listed on the main page under "Downloads". Both are necessary to target both platforms. Unzip and then launch the application. You should see something like Figure 11.1. If you do, you are ready to customize it for your app. First, we will customize for Windows, and then we will customize for Mac. If you wish to start with Mac (or simply not use Windows), just read the Mac section first and come back and adapt with the Windows steps. The customizations are identical except for location.

Figure 11.1. node-webkit blank Windows.

11.3.1 node-webkit Game Package

The image shown in 11.1 is what happens when node-webkit starts without a package to run. We now need to set up our game for node-webkit. For this, we will be reusing Crafty Pong from Chapter 3. Copy the entire game (html, js files, and audio files) over to the same directory as node-webkit (nw.exe for Windows or node-webkit.app for Mac).

Next, similar to the Chrome Web Store, create a package.json file. In that file, put this:

```
{
  "main": "index.html",
  "name": "com.example.craftypong,
  "description": "Crafty Pong",
  "window": {
    "toolbar": false,
    "width": 500,
    "height": 500,
    "min_width": 500,
    "min_height": 500,
    "max_width": 500,
    "max_height": 500
  }
}
```

Launch node-webkit (nw.exe for Windows or node-webkit.app for Mac). You should see something similar to Figure 11.2. Depending on your layout, the game might not look quite right since package.json forced a window size of 500 × 500, but that is small potatoes. This can be fixed in the index.html file. Proof of concept has been achieved.

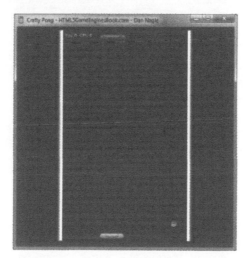

Figure 11.2. node-webkit Crafty Pong

Right now, you could zip up the entire directory and distribute it (after code obfuscation/minify techniques if desired, such as with UglifyJS). Every user with enough tech savviness to unzip files into their own directory can launch and play your game. That is good for development and testing, but that is usually not acceptable for a professional game. The next few sections show how to create installers for each platform and to tweak node-webkit to make it your own.

11.4   Windows Distribution

The downloaded Windows-based zip file comes with a handful of DLLs and executables. Most are related to graphics and GPU accelerations and should be included in your distribution (except nwsnapshot, which is not needed). The main file we are most concerned with is "nw.exe". That launches the app. There are a couple touch-ups needed.

11.4.1   Resource Editing

One downside to using precompiled binaries is the executable uses an incorrect icon. If you want to have your own icon, you can either recompile node-webkit (difficult) or directly edit the executable (easy). A utility I have been using for years is Resource Hacker located at http://www.angusj.com/resourcehacker/. See the screen shot at Figure 11.3 for how to replace the icon with your own.

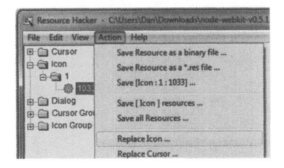

Figure 11.3. Replace icon with Resource Hacker.

Note that from the web page for Resource Hacker, the author states the project has been discontinued and, as of this writing, the latest version is 16 September 2011 [84]. My personal use over the years has shown that this utility is very stable. However, as it ages, and if there are no more updates, you may have to look for alternatives or not use precompiled node-webkit binaries and compile nw.exe from the source with the icon of your choosing.

The easiest and safest alternative would be to sidestep the issue altogether and build a "launcher" with the correct icon that simply launches nw.exe. The easiest utility to do this is probably AutoIt, located at http://www.autoitscript. com. It comes with an all-in-one installer that compiles to an exe with an icon of your choice and no dependencies. The compiled AutoIt script can be done in one line of code. However, if you wish to go this route, you may want to add a check to see that nw.exe actually exists before trying to launch it. See below for AutoIt code:

```
; AutoIt Script
If FileExists("nw.exe") Then
    Run ("nw.exe")
Else
    MsgBox(4096, "Error", "Could not find nw.exe!")
EndIf
```

Set up the AutoIt compiler to use the icon of your choice and then compile. Include your launcher app with the main app and point all related shortcuts to the launcher app so Windows uses the correct icon to refer to your app. The big downside to this technique is the app will still use the wrong icon when it is actually running, but that is the recommended stop-gap if you can no longer directly "hack" the resources inside nw.exe.

11.4.2 Enigma Virtual Box Alternative

node-webkit suggests Enigma Virtual Box (freeware [85]) as an alternative to building the full installer presented in the next section. What this utility does is bundle up all the related files into a single executable that can be run no-install.

This handy utility can solve a lot of use cases and may be a good enough solution for your HTML5 game. Note that this tool does not have an option to change the icon. You will still need to use a resource hacker for that.

11.4.3 Windows Installer

There are lots of install wizards. My personal preference on writing an installer that I have been using for years is Inno Setup located at http://www.jrsoftware. org/isinfo.php. When downloading, you will want the version that comes with Inno Script Studio. This is a powerful utility and a full tutorial is outside the scope of this book. The key component is that you want the entire directory. See the code in Listings 11.1 and 11.2.

```
{
; Script generated by the Inno Setup Script Wizard.
#define MyAppName "Crafty Pong"
#define MyAppVerName "Crafty Pong for Windows"
#define MyAppPublisher "Dan Nagle"
#define MyAppURL "http://html5gameenginesbook.com/"
#define MyAppExeName "craftypong.exe"
#define InstallDir "Crafty Pong"
#define GroupName "Crafty Pong"
#define MyDateTimeString GetDateTimeString('yyyy-mm-dd', '', '');

[Setup]
; NOTE: The value of AppId uniquely identifies this application.
AppId={{E7A1A2A9-B9D8-4AC4-9E57-5F81F478D1D5}}
AppName={#MyAppName}
```

```
AppVerName={#MyAppVerName}
AppPublisher={#MyAppPublisher}
AppPublisherURL={#MyAppURL}
AppSupportURL={#MyAppURL}
AppUpdatesURL={#MyAppURL}
DefaultDirName={pf}\CraftyPong
DefaultGroupName={#GroupName}
OutputDir=installer
OutputBaseFilename=CraftyPong{#MyDateTimeString}
SetupIconFile=resources\html5logo.ico
LicenseFile=resources\craftyponglicense.rtf
Compression=lzma2/ultra64
AlwaysRestart = "no"
```

Listing 11.1. Inno setup example.

```
[Languages]
Name: English; MessagesFile: compiler:Default.isl

[Tasks]
Name: desktopicon; Description: {cm:CreateDesktopIcon}; \
 GroupDescription: {cm:AdditionalIcons};

[Files]
Source: resources\*; DestDir: {app}; Flags: ignoreversion

[Icons]
Name: {group}\{#MyAppName}; Filename: {app}\{#MyAppExeName}
Name: {commondesktop}\{#MyAppName}; Filename: \
 {app}\{#MyAppExeName}; Tasks: desktopicon

[Icons]
Name: {group}\{#MyAppName}; Filename: {app}\{#MyAppExeName};
Name: {commondesktop}\{#MyAppName}; \
  Filename: {app}\{#MyAppExeName};  IconFilename: \
   {app}\html5logo.ico; Tasks: desktopicon

[Run]
Filename: {app}\{#MyAppExeName}; Description: \
 {cm:LaunchProgram,{#MyAppName}}; Flags: \
 nowait postinstall skipifsilent
```

Listing 11.2. Inno setup example.

1. The header part is fairly boilerplate except it is using GetDateTimeString. This fetches the current date to be appended to in the final installer file name, which is outputted in its own directory called "installer". This helps track versions. This is absolutely crucial when juggling multiple releases. Note that the game itself also should output a version number. By convention, a normal app's version is located in Help → About. A game should have an easy-to-find location on the main splash screen.

2. The generated installer is found in the "installer" directory. That is the
final binary that gets sent to the users to install and play the game.

3. Next, it grabs the entire "resources" directory. This is what gets installed.

4. Under "Tasks", it asks the user if they want a desktop icon for the app.
Many users get annoyed when icons are placed without asking. Placing
"Quicklaunch" icons is a similar process.

5. Finally, after installing, it asks the user if they wish to run the app.

Build the install package, and you are finished. You now have a desktop
HTML5 game that installs and runs like any normal offline game.

11.5   Mac Distribution

Mac distribution is easier than Windows distribution. Note that like Windows,
you could zip up the entire directory and just send that. If you wish to go
beyond zip files, the Mac standard for installers is DMG. The DMG framework
comes built in and can be executed with one line (shown later). The vast
majority of the effort is style tweaks to make the installer look nice. First,
we need to get our app inside "node-webkit.app", and then we will apply the
styles tweaks (DMG and icons).

11.5.1   node-webkit.app

A Mac ".app" is actually a normal directory with a special structure. You
can right-click an ".app" and click "Show Package Contents" to look inside.
Do this now with the baseline node-webkit.app. You will see a "Contents"
directory. Inside that directory, you will find:

Frameworks
    This holds the core frameworks that are used by node-webkit. It should
    be left alone.

info.plist
    This follows Apple guidelines to customize your app and make it your
    own. This file is in XML and should be edited to fit your needs.
    At minimum, "CFBundleIdentifier" should be changed to your own
    "com.example.myapp". CFBundleInfoDictionaryVersion should be your
    version. CFBundleName should be your app's name.

MacOS
    This contains the node-webkit executable that gets launched.

PkgInfo

The contents of this file simply states it is an Apple package.

Resources

Inside Resources, you have a directory called "app.nw". **That is where your actual game resides**. It is just like the zipped app.nw created for Windows except this is a normal uncompressed directory. Also, inside Resources is an icon set called "nw.icns" described next.

"nw.icns" is a collection of PNG images combined into a special icon format designed by Apple. It is similar to the classic Windows ".ico" format. Apple ships a utility called "iconutil" that can generate icns files. First, you need to create the icons in the required formats. These include:

Filename	Dimensions
icon_16.png	16 × 16
icon_16@2x.png	32 × 32
icon_32.png	32 × 32
icon_32@2x.png	64 × 64
icon_128.png	128 × 128
icon_128@2x.png	256 × 256
icon_256.png	256 × 256
icon_256@2x.png	512 × 512
icon_512.png	512 × 512
icon_512@2x.png	1024 × 1024

All of these should go in a separate directory called "nw.iconset". The suffix ".iconset" is important. Otherwise, iconutil will generate an error. From the parent directory of "nw.iconset", run this command to generate the icns file.

```
iconutil -c icns iconset
```

The file generated will be "nw.icns". That file should be placed in game.app → Contents → Resources. After copying it over, the icon of the app should change.

The app is finished. You could zip this up right now and distribute. The next section describes how to put together an installer. Most Mac apps use DMG files.

11.5.2 DMG File

DMG files are Apple disk images. They can be thought of as "iso" files often used to distribute CD/DVD images. The convenience of disk images is that internally they can use the HFS+ file system, a format developed by Apple for Mac OS X [86]. Creating a disk image to hold these contents before compressing makes them ideal to send over the internet to places that may not understand how to read the HFS+ system. While standard compression utilities, such as zip, may not properly capture all the miscellaneous permissions and other file aspects unique to HFS+, DMG does not have these limitations. The DMG archive itself is what gets compressed.

There are two ways to create a DMG to distribute your app (or perhaps a third way: purchasing one of the many DMG creation utilities). The first way is really easy, but not as professional. However, it may be sufficient for your target audience.

After your app is ready, run this command:

```
hdiutil create -format UDBZ -quiet \
 -srcfolder mygame.app mygame.dmg
```

"hdiutil" is the DMG generation utility included by Apple. The above command will generate a compressed, ready-to-go DMG with your app inside it. This one line concludes the first method. You could use this DMG file as-is and most users will recognize a .app inside and know to drag it to their Applications folder.

However, most professional developers like to go beyond that. Some have background images and include a link to the Application directory helping the user to drop the app there. A third party tool can help with this process, but this is how to do it manually.

Before beginning, a little discussion on strategy. Through personal experience, I have found there is simply no good way to fully automate the build process of a styled DMG. It would be nice to launch a compile script that accepts code and generates an .app inside a compressed DMG with the correct links and graphical enhancements. The middle step is too fuzzy. Therefore, this is the compromise I use: Instead of a full complete build process, I use a DMG "template." This template has everything ready to go. All it needs is the final compiled app to be pushed inside it and then compressed. Since it is part of the build process, this template is then checked into my Git source control just like everything else. It just happens to be a fairly big binary blob. Fortunately, once built, it changes very little.

With that, it is time to build our template.

1. Create a directory to represent the disk image.
   In this example, the directory will be called "installer".

2. Inside "installer" directory, place a shortcut to Applications.
   Open Finder. Navigate to your main drive's directory. Right-click Applications folder, and then select "Make Alias". A shortcut will be generated.

Drag to your installer directory and rename it to "Applications". This is the shortcut that the user will drag our app to.

3. Create a background for the DMG.
   There are no clear-cut guidelines for this. Personally, I use a 600 x 400 PNG. Inside the image, there should be some kind of indication telling the user to drag the app to the Applications shortcut. Often, this is represented by a big arrow.

4. Create subdirectory called ".background".
   This is the secret trick that builders use to bundle an image or anything else they want to not be directly viewable by the end-user. Finder does not display files or directories that start with a period, often called "dot files". As such, Finder will not let you do create a folder that starts with period. Launch Terminal and use the command "mkdir .background" to create the directory. This directory will not be viewable in Finder.

5. Move background image to .background subdirectory.
   In the Terminal, use "mv background.png .background/" to do this. The image file will disappear from the finder window.

6. Make a DMG from the installer.
   In the parent directory, run this command from Terminal.

```
hdiutil create installer.dmg -srcfolder installer/ \
  -format UDRW
```

This will create a writable DMG with the contents of the directory inside it.

7. Mount the DMG. Customize as you please.
   Right-click in the blank area and select "View Options". Customize the view. Some things you will want to do:

   (a) Always open in Icon View.

   (b) Change the background.
       You need to open another Finder and go to the absolute path of the .background directory to be able to drop it in the View Options window. With one Finder open, drag the image to the view options of the other Finder. Yes, it is a bit awkward.

   (c) Note the other View options in the menu bar.
       From here, you can hide things such as path and status bar.

8. Compress the DMG and make readonly.
   After unmounting, here is the Terminal command to do it:

```
hdiutil convert installer.dmg -format UDZO \
  -imagekey zlib-level=9 -o installer_final.dmg
```

Test out installer_final.dmg to make sure it behaves as you expect. This is the final installer that you can use to distribute your app on the internet. The intermediate file, installer.dmg, can be renamed to installertemplate.dmg and checked into your version control (such as Git) since it is now part of your build process. Swap files in and out of this DMG whenever there is a new release. If this DMG is a bit big for your liking, you can compress and uncompress it. Note that Git already uses compression.

11.6 Summary

In this chapter, we built native desktop distributions of our game. node-webkit did the heavy lifting of creating a manageable version of Chromium that can be used to help distribute our game. With this native distribution, we can feel comfortable that any end-user on a wide variety of machines can play our game. We also were able to lighten the game a bit (removing Modernizr and MP3s) because we know exactly what "browser" is playing our game. Of course, lighten may not be a good word. The trade-off was bundling an entire browser engine for essentially a couple megabytes of JavaScript and media files. Regardless, we now have another avenue of distribution to an extremely large medium (Macs and Windows desktops) that allows offline playing of our game and is not reliant on any app stores.

Node.js is a good development platform in its own right. If you would like to explore beyond JavaScript (having the game talk back to your "server"), research how having Node.js available in node-webkit can help you. Also, keep in mind that since node-webkit is based on Chromium, and Chromium has migrated from Webkit to Blink, the name of the project may change.

This concludes the distribution techniques. The next chapter is the final notes of what has been covered.

Chapter 12

Final Notes

This book covered a large slice of HTML5 game development. Starting in Part I, we learned high level concepts, tools for development, and how to build a small pong game. Then in Part II, we stopped reinventing the wheel by introducing game engines to take our examples further. We used four top game engines to build 4 different demos that could be played on all the major desktop and mobile platforms and learned a lot in the process. Then in Part III, we learned how to package our games to be placed in the top app markets and natively on the desktop so our users can find and play them however they please.

In summary, we learned development and distribution of HTML5 games. So, what could be missing? That is what this chapter covers.

12.1 Plugins

Whether officially or indirectly, many of the tools we used have a plugin system to extend functionality beyond the normal use. This section covers a few of them.

12.1.1 Crafty Modules

Crafty plugins are called "modules." They are spread around the web, but many can be found at the http://CraftyComponents.com/ website. One that you may be particularly interested in is the Box2D module since Crafty lacks its own full physics engine. To use a Crafty module, you may surround your game with module declarations or create a component.

12.1.2   Impact Plugins

Impact also has a pseudo plugins system (through its "inject()" method) to extend functionality. The home page for many plugins can be found at http://www.pointofimpactjs.com/, but directly searching the Impact forums is a good place as well.

The plugins will include instructions on how to install. In general, it usually involves creating a "plugins" subdirectory from your main "lib" directory and unzipping the plugin there. Then you can include the plugin in your "requires('plugins.myplugin')" code.

One Impact plugin you may wish to glance at is "impactplusplus" (or "impact++").

12.1.3   CocoonJS Extensions

We used CocoonJS to accelerate our JavaScript and package our HTML5 game into a standalone Android game. The CocoonJS services actually go beyond that in the form of "CocoonJS Extensions" located at http://wiki.ludei.com/cocoonjs:extensions. There are extensions available to allow access to various mobile internals not part of normal JavaScript, such as contacts, camera, ads, in-app purchasing, etc. Naturally, if you wish to make heavy use of CocoonJS extensions and acceleration, you will probably develop for mobile first (which is a good strategy anyway) and then target desktop second (if at all).

Some of the extensions require a premium account. Right now, premium accounts are free (like normal accounts). However, you must fill out an application and get approval. Note that the CocoonJS Extensions also work in DOM mode for normal web apps.

12.2   Desktop Stores

Mac and Windows both have app stores that weren't covered in this book. This is because both are fairly recent additions and fairly easy to bypass to sell the installer directly. However, they are available as another avenue to sell your game.

If you go this route, note that the Windows store has lots of interface guidelines that (for now) only Visual Studio 2012 can pass. Node-webkit will not pass. There is an Impact-oriented Windows bootstrap project located in GitHub at:
https://github.com/gamecook/super-jetroid-starter-kit

Take a look at that to see how to proceed. Note that JavaScript is a first-class citizen when developing for Windows 8, so there are no real barriers to HTML5. You will need to work through the style and approval process. The end result will be a lightweight app that internally calls on Windows 8's own IE rendering engine to power your app.

For the Mac App Store, node-webkit will not pass their guidelines either. The strategy here is the same as Windows Store: Use the desktop's native rendering engine. Take a look at https://github.com/maccman/macgap for a method to build your app to run natively as a WebView calling the Mac's rendering engine.

Note that the capability of your game is dependent on the browser the end user has installed, which usually means targeting the default OS version. Most of the engines should work fine with this strategy except perhaps Turbulenz because WebGL support is very weak in default Windows 8 IE.

12.3 Monetization

Throughout the entirety of this book, there has been little or no coverage on app monetization. The best way to earn money from your game is a complex decision that should be made very early. Therefore, it usually falls into the realm of "game design" while this book tries to focus on "game development." However, it is worth at least a mention.

There are many ways to monetize an app, but the most common methods include:

1. Sell the app directly.
   This is very straightforward, and it is the method that was assumed in this book. You write the app. When finished, you put it on the app store and sell it for X dollars. Usually, the app store takes around a 30% cut for itself.

2. Show ads.
   To do this, you would most likely sign up for an ad service, such as iAds or AdMob. A small slice of your app's screen is reserved for this ad network. There are tons of ad networks with varying methods of paying. Usually, there is a very small fee paid for number of "impressions", which is a count of how many times it is shown. Often, that number is in the many thousands and is not even a concern unless the app becomes really popular. There is a much larger fee paid if a user actually clicks/touches the ad. That can be an immediate payment of several cents and can add up quick.

3. In-App Purchases (or IAP).
   This is the business model of the "freemium" games. You give a game away for free. Premium enhancements, or perhaps shortcuts for the

game, require an in-app purchase. In-app purchases are also sometimes used to unlock a "lite" version of an app to a full version. Usually, the app store takes around a 30% cut for itself on IAP.

It is not uncommon to combine two revenue models. Often a "freemium" game also will have ads. A paid app could have IAP (in the style that many console games have "downloadable content" that costs extra). A paid game usually does not have ads. You could do that, but your users would probably revolt. Also, note that paid apps + IAP is not tolerated well on mobile either.

Regardless of the path you take, you should decide early. Most game engines have a way to support ads and IAPs.

12.4   Signing Off

This concludes the HTML5 Game Engines book. If you have any questions or comments, the support website is located at http://HTML5GameEnginesBook. com/.

Thank you for reading, and good luck with your game!

Tools Appendix

Important tools that aren't necessarily the focus of the book have been placed here. The appendix is intended to be read like another chapter, but with the liberty to simply skip tools you have already seen.

Android Studio

Android Studio was announced in early 2013 as the next generation of development tools for Android development. As of this writing, it is currently in early access preview and has a few bugs, but it is still far enough along that it can be used. By the time you receive this book, it will probably be a lot more stable and should be your first download for native development. Unlike the old Android SDK that uses Eclipse, Android Studio is based on IntelliJ IDEA [105]. The feature list is very promising.

Audacity

Audacity is a free audio editing tool available on all major platforms. It has numerous features, including recording live audio, mixing, splicing, and audio format conversion (Wav, MP3, OGG, ...).

Autodesk Maya

Maya is a commercial 3D computer graphics software used for animation and modeling. It is very feature rich and has been used for many high-budget films and computer games. For our purposes, it can be used to create 3D models that can be imported into the Turbulenz game engine.

AutoIt

AutoIt is a freeware scripting, automation, and GUI builder utility. It is notable in this book for its simple Basic-like syntax and compiling to a single executable with no dependencies.

Blender

Blender is free, open-source-3D modeling and texturing software. It has feature parity with some of the proprietary software packages. If you have looked at it in the past and got annoyed with the interface, take a look again. It has improved immensely in the past five years. The Turbulenz HTML5 engine can translate the .dae export format from Blender for use in 3D game development.

Bfxr

Bfxr is a handy utility for generating quick sound effects (such as jump, hit, open, etc.). It can be run online or as a standalone app. All sounds generated are yours to keep [23]. For those wanting to try to create a complete musical score, there is MuseScore available for all platforms.

Box2D

Box2D is a widely used, open source physics engine. If a game engine does not implement its own physics engine (such as Impact and Turbulenz), there is a good chance that Box2D will be available as a plugin or module.

CocoonJS

CocoonJS is a compiler and launcher developed by Ludei that allows packaging an HTML5-based app to be played and distributed on iOS and Android [69].

Cygwin

Cygwin is the first choice for Linux admins and enthusiasts for getting an encapsulated command prompt with access to their familiar Linux commands (grep, ls, tar, cat, and others) on a Windows-based machine. The installer has many packages available. Cygwin is free and maintained by Red Hat, Inc. [61].

Eclipse

Eclipse is the current IDE for writing native Android apps. The Android Development Toolkit (ADT) now comes with Eclipse bundled with it [29]. Some developers prefer Netbeans for Java development, but the official and most supported tools use Eclipse. Eclipse runs on both Windows and Mac.

Note that while ADT may be the tool of choice, the next generation of Android development will be Android Studio, which is currently in limited release. By the time you receive this book, Android Studio may have already superseded the Eclipse version.

Enigma Virtual Box

Enigma Virtual Box is freeware utility that can be used to consolidate an app with dependencies into a single-file portable executable app [85].

FileZilla

FileZilla is a widely used and frequently updated file transfer client. It is available on all platforms. It is most commonly used for FTP, but a less-often and more useful feature is SFTP, which is a secure file transfer protocol provided by OpenSSH. If you have Secure Shell (SSH) access to your server (fairly common), you can probably use SFTP to access your files and not need to bother with FTP accounts.

Git

Git is a free and open source software version control system developed by Linus Torvalds (creator of Linux) [24]. There are dozens of version control systems out there. All are good. Git is simply the most prevalent as it solves many of the problems with previous version control tools, and it is free and runs well on all platforms. Many IDEs have git support built in. Even if they don't, the Git Bash shell for Windows is excellent.

HTML5 Boilerplate

HTML5 Boilerplate is an all-in-one starting template to build a modern HTML5-based website. It includes many of the common libraries (jQuery, Modernizr, Normalize, etc.) and configurations (.htaccess) to build a site that leverages known best practices to support a wide range of browsers. It is intended to be downloaded and then adapted to suit your needs.

Inno Setup Studio

Inno Setup is my recommended tool for building Windows installers. It is very powerful (on parity with paid solutions), easy to use, and free for commercial use. You will want the "Studio" version when you download [26].

Instant Eyedropper/DigitalColor Meter.app

Instant Eyedropper for Windows will look at any pixel on your screen and copy the HEX, RGB, or HTML color code to your clip board. It sits in your system tray. Click and drag the magnifier to the point of interest. It is very handy. Mac comes with an equivalent utility called DigitalColor Meter. It is located in:
/Applications/Utilities/.

jQuery, jQuery UI, jQuery Mobile

jQuery is an excellent free JavaScript library. It abstracts all the odd idiosyncrasies of IE, Firefox, Chrome, etc. to a standard function. By favoring jQuerys functions over the normal standard JavaScript, your site will behave the same cross-platform as jQuery performs the cross-platform translations for you. As a bonus, you get a very nice selector engine and other very useful library functions. If this was a general-purpose web development book, then there would be anywhere from a dozen pages to an entire chapter dedicated just to jQuery. Over half of all websites use it [20]. This book is only really interested in HTML5 Canvas, which does not use DOM. However, you will probably want to build a normal DOM-based website to support your Canvas-based game, and to help you do this, you will probably want to use jQuery. There are numerous books and tutorials. The best resources are the jQuery websites themselves (http://jquery.com/ and http://jqueryui.com).

jQuery UI is jQuery plus bundled CSS libraries and images for added effects and other UI widgets, such as draggable, droppable, date picker, sliders, tabs, etc. There is a theme framework with lots of nice default themes, or you can roll your own [21].

jQuery Mobile is an extension of jQuery UI optimized for mobile devices. The usual events for desktop dont necessarily work for mobile devices. For example, "orientationchange" has been added. The design guidelines also have been reworked to be more responsive to tablets and phone sizes [22].

Legacy Browsers

Legacy Browsers are a must for testing. Portable Apps (http://PortableApps.com/) has old versions of Chrome (few) and Firefox (many) available as portable downloads and can run standalone in its own separate directory. This is very useful for testing previous versions as well as versions with no add-ons or some add-ons enabled. Opera USB (http://opera-usb.com) tracks portable versions of Opera.

For Internet Explorer, one tool is IETester (http://www.my-debugbar.com/wiki/IETester). It is an all-in-one tester for IE 6 through 9 (plus 10 if you are running Windows 8) though it has mediocre performance.

These Legacy Browser tools are Windows-only. Mac users can install these tools on their Windows Virtual Machine that they use for IE testing. Unfortunately, OS X is not allowed to be virtualized (outside of some special cases for OS X Server) [30]. Windows users will simply need to find a Mac to test Safari because as of version 6, Safari is no longer available on Windows [31].

MediaWiki

The software that powers Wikipedia is called MediaWiki [16]. It is free to download and install. Often, hosting providers have an auto-installer that can install it for you (though making it private is up to you). If you don't have a web server and don't wish to pay for one, there are many free private wiki sites. A wiki allows other designers to edit, upload files and graphics, roll back changes, be alerted on changes, link internally/externally to other pages, provide comments, and dozens of other very useful features. It is my recommend format for game design rather than just a static document.

Microsoft Visual Studio

Microsoft Visual Studio is the official IDE from Microsoft for developing applications for Windows. It is a nice IDE with numerous features that can fill an entire book itself. For our purposes, we are only concerned about Visual Studio's compiler. Turbulenz requires it as part of its build setup. Microsoft offers free (with registration) express editions that have access to the compiler.

Modernizr

Modernizr is a library that helps detect HTML5 compatibility and lets you degrade gracefully. It is covered in more detail on page 28.

Node.js

The easiest way to describe Node.js is "Server-side JavaScript." Whereas normal JavaScript runs on the client's browser, Node.js allows JavaScript to be written to web servers. It contains a package manager, a built-in web server, and more. Due to the nature of its design, it is highly scalable. Though not directly, node.js is used as part of Node-webkit, covered on page 160.

Open Game Art

Open Game Art http://opengameart.org/ is a site with lots of free game-related media with liberal licenses that can be used for your game project. Note that even though some media say it can be used for commercial purposes, I urge you not to do so unless you perform due diligence to verify the origin of the art for yourself. For open source and noncommercial purposes or tech demos, this site is probably a safe resource.

Paint.Net/Pixelmator

Paint.Net is similar to Photoshop except that it is free and has been reduced to the bare essentials. Sometimes less is more. I often find myself launching it more often than normal Photoshop. For Mac users, the equivalent is Pinta, though the Mac version requires Mono (.NET translation layer). A better low-cost commercial offering for Mac users is Pixelmator.

PhoneGap/Apache Cordova

Apache Cordova, the engine that powers PhoneGap by Adobe Systems, gets an extended section simply because it is so popular. It is a painless way to get HTML, CSS, and JavaScript apps to run standalone on an Android/iOS device, but unlike Ejecta and CocoonJS (the two recommended ways discussed in Part 3 of this book), it is not optimized for games and canvas, and it shows. App performance, particularly games, in general, is not very good with Apache Cordova. However, not every app requires game-engine level performance. If your app just uses DOM and is light on visuals, PhoneGap can get you pretty far.

To get your app running with PhoneGap, you need to download and install the Android SDK or use the recently released cloud-compiler. Apache Cordova is a library package that gets compiled with the native developer kit, which for Android is Eclipse bundled in with the Android SDK. Once Eclipse is running, import the PhoneGap sample Android project:

1. File → New → Project... (*not* "Android Project")

2. Android → Android Project from Existing Code

3. Set root to where you unzipped PhoneGap and import all the Android projects. Tell Eclipse to copy to your workspace.

4. Close the "_ACTIVITY_" project so Eclipse will stop complaining about errors.

5. Eclipse should now look like Figure 12.1.

Figure 12.1. Apache Cordova Eclipse.

Now, compile and run "cordovaExample" as-is. Your Android device should show something similar to Figure 12.2. If it does, your build environment is complete.

Figure 12.2. Apache Cordova Hello World.

As of this writing, Apache Cordova cannot handle an HTML5-based game. It will load, but the performance will be bad. It will be bad even on a recent, well-powered Android tablet. To give Cordova the best chance, use a lighter weight engine, such as the Crafty Pong project, and configure it to use DOM instead of Canvas. For a simple web app, Cordova works well. For an HTML5 game, at least for now, it does not.

Putty/SSH

Putty is a free SSH client for Windows. Mac users have SSH built in with Terminal. If you are developing a website, SSH is very useful for the tasks that are inefficient with web-based managers.

Python

Python is free, widely used, general purpose programming language. A version of it is included by default on Mac OS X and most Linux distributions. It is a very nice programming language with numerous uses, but for our purposes here, it is often used as part of a command-line build system, particularly Turbulenz and Heroku (for Facebook). Windows does not include Python by default, so it will need to be installed. Python is also available through Cygwin.

Resource Hacker

Resource Hacker is a freeware Windows utility for directly editing DLLs and executables. It supports functionality such as changing icons and sounds. This utility has been discontinued, but is still widely used [84].

Three.js

Three.js is an open source (MIT licensed) JavaScript library used to speed 3D graphics development with WebGL. It contains numerous features, such as scenes, animation, lighting, materials, shaders, cameras, etc. Three.js is not covered in this book because Turbulenz provides these features for us. However, if you wish to develop 3D closer to the metal than what Turbulenz provides, you should consider using three.js to help your development.

UglifyJS

UglifyJS is a JavaScript processor utility that can minify, obfuscate, or beautify JavaScript files. Turublenz uses it for compaction. It is often included through node.js packages.

VLC Media Player

VLC has nearly all audio and video codecs that you could want built in so it can play essentially everything thrown at it with no fuss. It is free and loads fast. It is necessary for building media-driven sites.

VMware Player/VMware Fusion/Parallels/Virtual Box

VMware Player is useful for testing your app on operating systems other than your development station. It is far easier to keep a virtual machine to test your various use-cases than a regular machine. Create a snapshot of the scenario you want to test and rollback when you need to test again. Parallels and Fusion are Mac virtualization tools. VMware Player is for Windows, and Virtual Box is available on both.

VMware Player does not support snapshots, but you can get around this deficiency by simply making a copy of the directory where your virtual machine resides (vmdk, vmx, etc.). Note that as of version 5, VMware Player (Windows) is no longer free for noncommercial use unless you purchase a copy of Fusion Pro [25]. Virtual Box is still free [28].

If you are running a Mac, then some form of virtualization is a must if you wish to test IE (or use Boot Camp). Even if you use portable editions of legacy browsers, a virtual machine can still be useful for capturing complex development environments.

Web Servers

WAMP is an easy way to get a development web server with Apache, MySQL, and PHP on Windows. MAMP is an equivalent package for Mac. XAMPP is available for both Windows and Mac with a lot more features than just Apache+MySQL+PHP, but it isn't as easy to use. This book recommends WAMP for Windows and MAMP for Mac.

There is a $20 Apple-supported Mac App Store app for Mountain Lion and later, called "OS X Server," that will get a web server running. It is not really suitable for quick development as it is oriented more toward a

Mac monoculture enterprise setup: A local intranet, iCal management, user accounts, a group Wiki, etc. If you do wish to go that route, note that your server root files will be located at:
/Library/WebServer/Documents

Internet Information Services (IIS) is the Microsoft-supported web server built in to Windows (but not enabled). PHP (required for Impact development) does not come by default, but it can be installed for free as a plugin from http://php.iis.net/. IIS's default server root is C:\Inetpub\wwwroot . The rather complex setup to get PHP working is presented on page 35.

Also, note that if all you need is a simple HTTP server to serve files, Python has one built in. Any directory can be made in a web directory listing. Navigate to the directory and run this command:

```
python -m SimpleHTTPServer
```

You will then have a very simple HTTP server running for that location on port 8000. Go to http://127.0.0.1:8000 to view it. All Macs and most Linux distributions ship with a version of Python.

Xcode

Xcode is provided by Apple for writing iOS or Mac apps. There are lots of third-party tools that often can bypass Xcode for Mac desktop development, but it will be needed when you are ready to distribute iOS apps.

Bibliography

[1] The History of Java Technology. Oracle. http://www.oracle.com/ technetwork/java/javase/overview/javahistory-index-198355.html (accessed May 11, 2013).

[2] Learn About Java Technology. Oracle. http://www.java.com/en/about/ (accessed May 11, 2013).

[3] Java Development Guide for Mac. Mac Developer Library. 20 October 2010. https://developer.apple.com/library/mac/documentation/ Java/Conceptual/Java14Development/00-Intro/JavaDevelopment.html (accessed May 11, 2013).

[4] The History of Flash. Adobe. http://www.adobe.com/macromedia/events/ john_gay/page04.html (accessed May 11, 2013).

[5] Flash to Focus on PC Browsing and Mobile Apps; Adobe to More. Adobe Featured Blogs. 9 November 2011. http://blogs.adobe.com/conversations/ 2011/11/flash-focus.html (accessed May 11, 2013).

[6] WHATWG. 29 April 2013. HTML Living Standard. http://http://whatwg. org/html (accessed April 29, 2013).

[7] W3C. 17 December 2012. HTML Living Standard. http://www.w3.org/ TR/html5/ (accessed April 29, 2013).

[8] HTML5 Living Standard (Timers). 2013. http://www.whatwg.org/specs/ web-apps/current-work/multipage/timers.html (accessed May 4, 2013).

[9] W3C. 24 December 1999. HTML 4.01 Specification. http://www.w3.org/ TR/html401 (accessed April 29, 2013).

[10] W3C. 1 August 2002. XHTML(TM) 1.0 The Extensible HyperText Markup Language (Second Edition). http://www.w3.org/TR/xhtml1/ (accessed April 29, 2013).

[11] W3C. 22 July 2004. XHTML 2.0. W3C Working Draft http://www.w3. org/TR/2004/WD-xhtml2-20040722/ (accessed April 29, 2013).

[12] HTML Living Standard. WHATWG. 14 August 2013. XHTML 2.0. W3C Working Draft http://www.whatwg.org/specs/web-apps/current-work/multipage/introduction.html#is-this-html5 (accessed August 15, 2013).

[13] WHATWG. 23 February 2013. FAQ - WHATWG Wiki http://wiki.whatwg.org/wiki/FAQ (accessed April 29, 2013).

[14] WHATWG. 19 January 2011. HTML is the new HTML5 http://blog.whatwg.org/html-is-the-new-html5 (accessed April 29, 2013).

[15] W3C. 18 November 2010. Web SQL Database http://www.w3.org/TR/webdatabase/ (accessed April 29, 2013).

[16] MediaWiki. 20 March 2013. Project:About. http://www.mediawiki.org/wiki/Project:About (accessed April 29, 2013).

[17] Microsoft. 2013. Internet Explorer 9 system requirements. http://windows.microsoft.com/en-us/internet-explorer/products/ie-9/system-requirements (accessed April 29, 2013).

[18] Microsoft. 2013. Windows XP SP3 and Office 2003 Support Ends April 8, 2014. http://www.microsoft.com/en-us/windows/endofsupport.aspx (accessed April 29, 2013).

[19] Tim Berners-Lee. http://www.w3.org/People/Berners-Lee/ (accessed April 29, 2013).

[20] Matthias Gelbmann. 13 August 2012. jQuery now runs on every second website http://w3techs.com/blog/entry/jquery_now_runs_on_every_second_website (accessed April 29, 2013).

[21] jQuery UI. http://jqueryui.com/ (accessed April 29, 2013).

[22] jQuery Mobile. http://jquerymobile.com/ (accessed April 29, 2013).

[23] Bfxr. http://www.bfxr.net/ (accessed April 29, 2013).

[24] Git. Getting Started - A Short History of Git. http://git-scm.com/book/en/Getting-Started-A-Short-History-of-Git (accessed April 29, 2013).

[25] VMware. VMware Player. http://www.vmware.com/products/player/ (accessed April 29, 2013).

[26] Inno Setup. Jordan Russell. http://www.jrsoftware.org/isinfo.php (accessed July 7, 2013).

[27] New Channels for Firefox Rapid Releases. The Mozilla Blog. 13 April 2011. http://blog.mozilla.org/blog/2011/04/13/new-channels-for-firefox-rapid-releases/ (accessed May 4, 2013).

[28] Oracle. Oracle VM VirtualBox - Welcome to VirtualBox.org. https://www.
      virtualbox.org/ (accessed April 29, 2013).

[29] Android SDK. Get the Android SDK. http://developer.android.com/sdk/
      index.html (accessed April 29, 2013).

[30] Apple. Software License Agreements. http://www.apple.com/legal/sla/
      (accessed April 29, 2013).

[31] Apple. 16 April 2013. Apple security updates. http://support.apple.com/
      kb/HT1222 (accessed April 29, 2013).

[32] Apple.   5   May   2013.   http://developer.apple.com/library/ios/
      documentation/userexperience/conceptual/mobilehig/IconsImages/
      IconsImages.html (accessed May 5, 2013).

[33] The Hobbit, About The Film. 2012. http://www.thehobbit.com/hfr3d/
      faq.html (accessed July 30, 2013).

[34] HTML5 Living Standard (Canvas). 2013. http://www.whatwg.org/specs/
      web-apps/current-work/multipage/the-canvas-element.html (accessed May
      4, 2013).

[35] DisplayObject - AS3. Adobe. 2013. http://help.adobe.com/en_US/
      FlashPlatform/reference/actionscript/3/flash/display/DisplayObject.
      html (accessed May 4, 2013).

[36] Mobile Internet traffic gaining fast on desktop Internet traffic.
      CNET. 3 December 2012. http://news.cnet.com/8301-1023_3-57556943-93/
      mobile-internet-traffic-gaining-fast-on-desktop-internet-traffic/ (accessed
      May 4, 2013).

[37] Report: Mobile   Traffic   To   Local   Sites   Growing   Faster
      Than   To   Total   Internet,   Now   At   27   Percent.   Search
      Engine   Land.   3   May   2013.   http://searchengineland.com/
      report-mobile-traffic-to-local-sites-growing-faster-than-total-internet-now-
      at-27-percent-158139 (accessed May 4, 2013).

[38] Smartphones Outsell Dumbphones for First Time, Report Says. 26
      April 2013. ABC News. http://abcnews.go.com/blogs/technology/2013/
      04/smartphones-outsell-dumbphones-for-first-time-report-says/ (accessed
      May 4, 2013).

[39] Samsung GALAXY S4. 2013. Samsung. http://www.samsung.com/global/
      microsite/galaxys4/ (accessed May 4, 2013).

[40] StatCounter Global Stats. April 2013. StatCounter. http://gs.statcounter.
      com/ (accessed May 4, 2013).

[41] 300 million users and move to WebKit. 12 February 2013. Opera. http://my. opera.com/ODIN/blog/300-million-users-and-move-to-webkit (accessed May 4, 2013).

[42] JavaScriptCore. 06 March 2013. Hosted by Apple. http://trac.webkit.org/ wiki/JavaScriptCore (accessed May 4, 2013).

[43] V8 JavaScript Engine. Google Project Hosting. http://code.google.com/ p/v8/ (accessed May 4, 2013).

[44] Blink. The Chromium Projects. http://www.chromium.org/blink (accessed May 4, 2013).

[45] Blink: A rendering engine for the Chromium project. The Chromium Blog. http://blog.chromium.org/2013/04/blink-rendering-engine-for-chromium. html (accessed May 4, 2013).

[46] App Store Review Guidelines. Apple. 2013. https://developer.apple.com/ appstore/resources/approval/guidelines.html (accessed May 4, 2013).

[47] IE7 Is Coming This Month...Are you Ready?. IEBlog. 6 October 6 2006. http://blogs.msdn.com/b/ie/archive/2006/10/06/ ie7-is-coming-this-month_2e002e002e00_are-you-ready_3f00_.aspx (accessed May 4, 2013).

[48] Windows Phone Features. Microsoft. 2013. http://www.windowsphone. com/en-us/features/all (accessed May 4, 2013).

[49] Release Early, Release Often. The Chromium Blog. 22 July 2010. http:// blog.chromium.org/2010/07/release-early-release-often.html (accessed May 4, 2013).

[50] MP3 Licensing Royalty Rates. Technicolor. 2009. http://mp3licensing. com/royalty/ (accessed May 4, 2013).

[51] Vorbis.com:FAQ. Xiph.Org. 2009. http://www.vorbis.com/faq/ (accessed May 4, 2013).

[52] NES Specifications. Everynes. 2004. http://nocash.emubase.de/everynes. htm (accessed May 4, 2013).

[53] Conditional comments. Microsoft. 21 November 2012. http://msdn. microsoft.com/en-us/library/ie/hh801214%28v=vs.85%29.aspx (accessed May 5, 2013).

[54] Louis Stowasser. 28 February 2013. http://louisstowasser.com/ (accessed May 5, 2013).

[55] Crafty - JavaScript Game Engine. November 2012. http://craftyjs.com/ (accessed May 5, 2013).

[56] Safari Web Content Guide. Handling Events. 19 September 2012. http://developer.apple.com/library/ios/documentation/AppleApplications/Reference/SafariWebContent/HandlingEvents/HandlingEvents.html (accessed May 5, 2013).

[57] CreateJS Blog. 1 May 2013. http://blog.createjs.com/ (accessed May 5, 2013).

[58] Open Source — Adobe and HTML. Adobe. 2013. http://html.adobe.com/opensource/ (accessed May 5, 2013).

[59] LimeJS HTML5 Game Framework. Digital Fruit. 10 January 2013. http://www.limejs.com/ (accessed May 5, 2013).

[60] Web Design Services — Digital Fruit. Digital Fruit. http://www.digitalfruit.ee (accessed May 5, 2013).

[61] Cygwin. 22 April 2013. http://www.cygwin.com/ (accessed May 5, 2013).

[62] Google Developers. Closure Tools. 18 May 2012. https://developers.google.com/closure/ (accessed May 5, 2013).

[63] Impact - HTML5 Canas & JavaScript Game Engine. 2013. http://impactjs.com/ (accessed May 5, 2013).

[64] Chrome Web Store: a solution in search of a problem?. Ars Technica. 9 December 2010. http://arstechnica.com/business/2010/12/thoughts-on-the-chrome-store-does-the-web-need-an-app-delivery-channel/ (accessed May 5, 2013).

[65] Developer registration fee. Chrome. 16 November 2011. https://support.google.com/chrome_webstore/answer/187591?hl=en (accessed May 5, 2013).

[66] Google plans to dump Adobe CSS tech to make Blink fast, not rich. Ars Technica. 27 January 2014. http://arstechnica.com/information-technology/2014/01/google-plans-to-dump-adobe-css-tech-to-make-blink-fast-not-rich/ (accessed Feb 2, 2014).

[67] Ejecta - Impact. 2013. http://impactjs.com/ejecta (accessed May 5, 2013).

[68] Whos Winning, iOS or Android? All the Numbers, All in One Place. Time. 16 April 2013. http://techland.time.com/2013/04/16/ios-vs-android/ (accessed May 5, 2013).

[69] CocoonJS. Ludei. 2013. http://www.ludei.com/tech/cocoonjs (accessed May 5, 2013).

[70] Alexa Top 500 Global Sites. Alexa Internet, Inc. 7 May 2013. http://www.alexa.com/topsites (accessed May 7, 2013).

[71] Facebook and Heroku: an even easier way to get started. Facebook Developer Blog. 15 September 2011. https://developers.facebook.com/blog/post/558/ (accessed May 7, 2013).

[72] WebGL - OpenGL ES 2.0 for the Web. Khronos Group. 2013. http://www.khronos.org/webgl (accessed May 7, 2013).

[73] OpenGL ES - The Standard for Embedded Accelerated 3D Graphics. Khronos Group. 2013. http://www.khronos.org/opengles/ (accessed May 7, 2013).

[74] Using Audio - Multimedia Programming Guide. iOS Developer Library. 1 September 2010. http://developer.apple.com/library/ios/documentation/AudioVideo/Conceptual/MultimediaPG/UsingAudio/UsingAudio.html (accessed May 7, 2013).

[75] Ejecta Integrating Impact Games. Impact. 2013. http://impactjs.com/ejecta/integrating-impact-games (accessed May 7, 2013).

[76] Apple Core Audio Format Specification 1.0. Mac Developer Library. 12 October 2011. https://developer.apple.com/library/mac/documentation/MusicAudio/Reference/CAFSpec/CAF_spec/CAF_spec.html (accessed May 8, 2013).

[77] Windows 8 Product Guide for Developers. Dev Center - Windows Store apps. Microsoft. 2013. http://msdn.microsoft.com/en-us/windows/apps/hh852650 (accessed May 8, 2013).

[78] Start Developing iOS Apps Today: Set Up. iOS Developer Library. Apple. 2013. https://developer.apple.com/library/ios/referencelibrary/GettingStarted/RoadMapiOS/chapters/GetToolsandInstall.html (accessed May 11, 2013).

[79] App Store Submission Tutorial. iOS Developer Library. Apple. 23 March 2013. http://developer.apple.com/library/ios/documentation/ToolsLanguages/Conceptual/YourFirstAppStoreSubmission/TestYourApponManyDevicesandiOSVersions/TestYourApponManyDevicesandiOSVersions.html (accessed May 11, 2013).

[80] Prepare for App Store Submission. iOS Developer Library. Apple. 23 March 2013. https://developer.apple.com/library/ios/referencelibrary/ GettingStarted/RoadMapiOS/chapters/RM_DevelopingForAppStore/ DevelopingForAppStore/DevelopingForAppStore.html (accessed May 11, 2013).

[81] Google: 900 Million Android Activations To Date. IGN. 15 May 2013. http://www.ign.com/articles/2013/05/15/ google-900-million-android-activations-to-date (accessed May 16, 2013).

[82] Live from Google I/O: Mo screens, mo goodness. Google Official Blog. 15 May 2013. http://googleblog.blogspot.com/2013/05/ live-from-google-io-mo-screens-mo.html (accessed May 18, 2013).

[83] rogerwang / node-webkit. GitHub. 27 April 2013. https://github.com/ rogerwang/node-webkit (accessed May 18, 2013).

[84] Resource Hacker Home Page. Angus Johnson. 16 September 2011. http:// www.angusj.com/resourcehacker/ (accessed July 19, 2013).

[85] Enigma Virtual Box. The Enigma Protector. 2013. http://enigmaprotector. com/en/aboutvb.html (accessed July 19, 2013).

[86] Archived - Mac OS: About Mac OS Extended Volume Hard Drive Format or HFS+. Apple. 10 May 2012. http://support.apple.com/kb/ht1604 (accessed May 21, 2013).

[87] Signing Your Applications. Android Developers. http://developer.android. com/tools/publishing/app-signing.html (accessed May 23, 2013).

[88] Creating an installable Android .apk. Ludei. http://wiki.ludei.com/ cocoonjs:androidapk (accessed May 23, 2013).

[89] XAMPP for Windows FAQ. Apache Friends. 17 January 2010. http:// www.apachefriends.org/en/faq-xampp-windows.html#vista (accessed May 26, 2013).

[90] Joseph Juran, 103, Pioneer in Quality Control, Dies. New York Times. 3 March 2008. http://www.nytimes.com/2008/03/03/business/03juran.html? _r=0 (accessed May 26, 2013).

[91] Turbulenz Engine Goes Open Source. James Austin. 2 May 2013. http://news.turbulenz.com/post/49430669886/ turbulenz-engine-goes-open-source (accessed May 31, 2013).

[92] Python2orPython3. Python Wiki. 9 March 2013. http://wiki.python.org/ moin/Python2orPython3 (accessed May 31, 2013).

[93] TypeScript. Microsoft. 2012. http://www.typescriptlang.org/ (accessed June 1, 2013).

[94] Turbulenz Platform. Turbulenz 0.26.1 documentation. 2013. http://docs. turbulenz.com/platform_overview.html (accessed June 29, 2013).

[95] Microsoft shows off WebGL, touch-capable features in Internet Explorer 11. Ars Technica. 26 June 2013. http://arstechnica.com/business/2013/06/ microsoft-shows-off-webgl-touch-capable-features-in-internet-explorer-11/ (accessed June 29, 2013).

[96] python(1) Mac OS X Manual Page. Apple. 10 Aug 2008. https://developer.apple.com/library/mac/documentation/Darwin/ Reference/ManPages/man1/python.1.html (accessed June 29, 2013).

[97] Dart: Structured web apps. The dartlang website. http://www.dartlang. org/ (accessed June 29, 2013).

[98] CoffeeScript. CoffeeScript web site. http://coffeescript.org/ (accessed June 29, 2013).

[99] COLLADA - Digital Asset and FX Exchange Schema. Khronos Group. 2013. https://collada.org/ (accessed June 29, 2013).

[100] The Physics2DDevice Object. Turbulenz 0.26.1 documentation. 2013. http://docs.turbulenz.com/jslibrary_api/physics2ddevice_api.html (accessed June 29, 2013).

[101] Box2D v2.2.0 User Manual. Box2D.org. 2011 Erin Catto. http://www. box2d.org/manual.html (accessed June 29, 2013).

[102] The Draw2DSprite Object.Turbulenz 0.26.1 documentation. 2013. http: //docs.turbulenz.com/jslibrary_api/draw2d_api.html (accessed June 29, 2013).

[103] The GraphicsDevice Object.Turbulenz 0.26.1 documentation. 2013. http: //docs.turbulenz.com/jslibrary_api/graphicsdevice_api.html (accessed June 29, 2013).

[104] Chrome 28 Blinks. Computer World. 2013 Jul 11. http://www. computerworld.com/s/article/9240713/Chrome_28_Blinks (accessed July 15, 2013).

[105] Getting Started with Android Studio. Android Developers. 2013 Jul. http://developer.android.com/sdk/installing/studio.html (accessed July 18, 2013).

Index

Printed and bound by CPI Group (UK) Ltd, Croydon, CR0 4YY

22/10/2024

01777624-0007